D. JAMES KENNEDY MINISTRIES

LET FREEDOM
Ring

Edited by
Jerry Newcombe, D. Min.

D. JAMES
KENNEDY
MINISTRIES

Fort Lauderdale, FL

Let Freedom Ring

Edited by Jerry Newcombe, D. Min.

ISBN: 978-1-929626-79-3

Cover and Interior Design: Roark Creative, www.roarkcreative.com

Printed in the United States of America.

Published by:

D. James Kennedy Ministries
P.O. Box 11786
Fort Lauderdale, FL 33339
1-800-988-7884
DJKM.org
letters@djkm.org

CONTENTS

For freedom Christ has set us free; stand firm therefore, and do not submit again to a yoke of slavery. . . . For you were called to freedom, brothers. Only do not use your freedom as an opportunity for the flesh, but through love serve one another.

GALATIANS 5:1, 13

FOREWORD
by Frank Wright

One of the seminal principles of Scripture is that revival begins with remembering. We see this in Jesus' letter to the church at Ephesus, recorded in the second chapter of Revelation. After commending the church for its patient endurance, Jesus says:

> But I have this against you, that you have aban-
> doned the love you had at first. Remember therefore
> from where you have fallen; repent, and do the works
> you did at first. If not, I will come to you and remove
> your lampstand from its place, unless you repent
> (Revelation 2:4-5).

In our day, we need look no further than the morning paper or your favorite news website to see a world seemingly in chaos—one in a headlong flight from any notion of Biblical morality or ethics; which begs some troubling questions. How do we get back from here? Is there hope for America once again becoming a nation under God?

As a nation, we need revival like few other times in our history. Such revival is, of course, a sovereign work of the Holy Spirit of God. Yet, Jesus says the place for us to begin is by remembering.

A good place to start is by remembering the Providence of God and the godly heritage that is ours because of the faithful men and women who have gone before us. We need to remember that America was birthed in the hearts of men and women who loved God, trusted Jesus Christ as Savior and Lord, and risked their lives to establish a nation to advance the Christian faith—all to the glory of God.

The authors contributing the chapters that follow walk us from the heights of God's providential care to the stark realities of a nation that has forgotten God. They show us the genius of the American Experiment and the contemporary threats that seek to undo the blessing of liberty.

Let Freedom Ring is not some Pollyannaish exercise in denying reality. It calls us first to consider the heights from which we have fallen. It then calls us to remember that America's destiny is inextricably linked to the character of her leaders. At each crucial turning point in our nation's history we find statesmen who believed in the principles of the Bible and relied wholeheartedly on the favor and Providence of God to carry them to victory against overwhelming odds. It calls us also to remember that:

> *The eyes of the Lord run to and fro throughout the*
> *whole earth, to give strong support to those whose*
> *heart is blameless toward Him* (2 Chronicles 16:9).

In the end, *Let Freedom Ring* is dedicated to the idea that America will not be transformed by the next set of laws or by the next business innovation, but with the strong support of God, it will be transformed by the next generation of leaders whose hearts are truly His.

The Cycle of Nations

by William J. Federer

And all that generation also were gathered to their fathers. And there arose another generation after them who did not know the LORD or the work that he had done for Israel.

JUDGES 2:10

Founding father George Mason, a delegate to the Constitutional Convention, said on August 22, 1787: "As nations cannot be rewarded or punished in the next world, they must be in this. By an inevitable chain of causes and effects, Providence punishes national sins, by national calamities."

From rags to riches to rags to riches: Is our nation following the same cyclical path as a father who sacrifices to provide prosperity for his son, only to have that son squander the wealth, so the grandson ends up having to sacrifice to provide prosperity for his son, only to have that son squander it?

Alas, the cycle of nations—from King Solomon's realm, to the Babylonian kingdom, to the Roman Empire, history is replete with examples of nations that struggled in their infancy, then reached unprecedented wealth and glory only to squander away their inheritance.

This tendency for history to repeat itself can be observed in the nation of Israel as chronicled in the book of Judges. Before they entered the Promised Land, they made a covenant with God and were blessed; then they backslid by worshiping the gods of other nations; then prophets called them to repentance. When they didn't repent, judgment came; then they repented and were delivered by Joshua, Gideon, Samson, and others. Then they renewed their covenant with

God and were blessed, beginning the cycle all over again.

America has had its own cycles to major and minor degrees. For example, after the signing of the Declaration of Independence, which was like a covenant as it refers to God four times, our nation was blessed. Then "prophets" arose calling us to repent of slavery, such as the abolitionist societies and courageous leaders such as Benjamin Franklin, who, after signing the Constitution, became the first president of the first anti-slavery society in America.

When our nation didn't repent, the judgment of the Civil War came, and more than 600,000 people died. In his Second Inaugural Address on March 4, 1865, President Lincoln said: "If we shall suppose that American slavery is one of those offenses which . . . He now wills to remove . . . as was said three thousand years ago, so still it must be said 'the judgments of the Lord are true and righteous altogether.'" Then our nation repented and "deliverers" such as Lincoln preserved the Union. We renewed our covenant with God, establishing an annual National Day of Thanksgiving to God in 1863, and placed "In God We Trust" on our national coinage in 1865. Then our country was blessed, and the cycle began all over again.

Today, we see a nation that is trying to force men into ladies' rooms; that aborts about a million unborn babies a year; and that is denying many Americans our first liberty—religious liberty. Yes, there has been immorality before, but today it seems to be on such a wide scale that it makes one blush. The Bible speaks of those who "glory in their shame." What a description of our times.

Note what was said by our nation's second First Lady. Abigail Adams, the wife of President John Adams and the mother of President John Quincy Adams, wrote a letter to her friend Mercy Warren during the Revolutionary War on November 5, 1775: "Is it possible that he whom no moral obligations bind, can have any real Good Will towards Men? Can he be a patriot who, by an openly vicious conduct, is undermining the very bonds of Society, corrupting the Morals of Youth, and by his bad example injuring the very Country he professes to patronize more than he can possibly compensate by intrepidity, Generosity and honour? The Scriptures tell us 'righteousness exalteth a Nation.'"

In light of all these things, what a delight it is to be able to recommend this book of essays compiled by Jerry Newcombe for D. James Kennedy Ministries. Here we find a look at our nation's unmistakable Judeo-Christian roots. We also find an explanation of the turning point in church-state understandings—a nation that is "one nation under God" is now swiftly moving away from God. We see the dire consequences of that movement, including the fact that in a nation founded by Christians for religious liberty (which was then extended to all), Christians are presently losing their religious liberty. We may well ask: What can we do about this? Is there any hope for America?

Included here are essays by a number of distinguished contributors: John Sorensen, president of Evangelism Explosion International, looks at the source of our hope for America. Peter Lillback, president of Providence Forum and president of Westminster Theological Seminary, comments on America's Christian roots. Former Congressman John Hostettler, senior executive director of the D. James Kennedy Center for Christian Statesmanship, writes of the genius of the Constitution. I, William J. Federer, write about the misunderstanding of church and state relations. David Gibbs, III, president of the National Center for Life and Liberty, apprises us on threats to religion in our time. D. James Kennedy and co-author Jerry Newcombe, sound the alarm on the major moral crisis of our day—the problem of abortion. Linda W. Smith, president of the D. James Kennedy Center for Christian Leadership, comments on another serious problem, that of incarceration. Jerry Newcombe, columnist and senior producer at D. James Kennedy Ministries, shows America's need for God. Frank Wright, president and chief executive officer of D. James Kennedy Ministries, concludes with a hopeful message for a new era of cultural engagement in America.

The question for us today is: Where is America in the cycle of nations? These essays by various authors show the good, the bad, and the challenges ahead. As the classic hymn, "My Country 'Tis of Thee," notes: "Let freedom ring!"

CHAPTER 1

Is There Any Hope for America?

by John Sorensen

The light shines in the darkness, and the darkness has not overcome it.
JOHN 1:5

America has certainly changed. But it yields a question . . . what happened? America is not the nation it once was at its founding. Sadly, we're not the nation we were 30, 20, even 10 years ago. And not only has it changed, but it's still changing, and the pace of change is picking up speed almost daily. Let me give you just a few examples to document America's plummeting moral decline:

1. We aren't getting married like we used to. About 50 percent of Americans over 18 are married, compared with 72 percent in 1960.[1]

2. The so-called "nones"—people without any religious affiliation—is up five percent since 2008 and now sits at 20 percent of the adult population.[2]

3. Around 1 million tiny human beings are killed each
   year by abortion, robbing the very least among us of
   their very first birthday.[3]

As Dr. D. James Kennedy, my spiritual mentor, once said to me,
"We're no longer on the slippery slope; we're over the edge hanging
on by our fingernails."

No, the trends are not good. Evangelical philosopher, Francis
Schaeffer, warned more than 30 years ago that secular values had already
displaced America's longstanding Judeo-Christian moral tradition.
Speaking in 1982, two years before his death, Dr. Schaeffer listed the
moral failings in Western society—pornography, the breakdown of the
family, abortion, infanticide, and euthanasia—but strongly emphasized
that all these things are just symptoms of something much more
fundamental, a much deeper problem as he explained:

> All of these things and many more are only the
> results. We may be troubled with the individual
> thing, but in reality we are missing the whole thing
> if we do not see each of these things and many more
> as only symptoms of the deeper problem. And that is
> the change in our society, a change in our country, a
> change in the Western world from a Judeo-Christian
> consensus to a Humanistic one.[4]

Is There Any Hope?

America is much further down the road than Francis Schaeffer or
D. James Kennedy could have imagined. After all, who could possibly
have conceived just two years ago that our nation's moral debate would
turn on whether to open bathrooms and locker rooms to confused or
predatory people of the opposite sex? But that is where we are, and that
raises the obvious question. Is there hope left for America? Is it possible
that our nation, which is now celebrating in its laws open rebellion

against God, will correct course and become, once more, a city set upon a hill—a beacon of hope to the rest of the world? The answer quite simply, I believe, is **yes.** That is what Evangelism Explosion is working and praying for every day. Its mission is to supply that which is most needed and, frankly, too often excluded from the life of our nation—including the halls of Washington, D. C.—namely, faith in God and His Son Jesus Christ.

Senator James Lankford of Oklahoma was the recipient of the 2015 Distinguished Christian Statesman Award, given annually by the D. James Kennedy Center for Christian Statesmanship (a sister ministry of Evangelism Explosion, both being started by the same founder) to honor individuals who combine excellence in public service with character and faith in God. Says Lankford:

> Many people have written Washington, D. C. off and say D. C. is a dark place and far from God, and godless people are there. And I always laugh and say at the very end in Sodom and Gomorrah, God was calling people out; but that's not what He's doing. He's still sending people in to Washington, D. C. And, quite frankly, it's very consistent with His character; if it's a dark place, God can send light there.[5]

How About the Experts

We live in a day and age when "experts" have many ideas about what people need to live in this country and in this world. Yet, the truth is that they have no actual answers for the darkness that creeps into our lives. We have seen many recent tragedies of nature, including devastating earthquakes, tsunamis, and hurricanes. In the midst of such difficulties, what real hope do these "experts" offer? And it is not just the darkness that comes from physical challenges and the loss of hope, but also there is a moral darkness that continues to creep across our land. To see it, you need only to look at the movies that

Hollywood produces and celebrates. Read Romans Chapter 1 and it is really clear what is going on.[6]

In the midst of this, Christians seem to have become more and more introverted. Or, at least, our introversion has become more and more obvious. We have never possessed more money, more time, more tools, more talent, more resources, and more people to carry the light of the Gospel throughout this land and to the ends of the earth than we have right now. Yet, we seem to be moving backwards in our ability and desire to create bridges over which to carry the Gospel:

- A growing number of our church members will live their whole lives next to neighbors whom they will never meet,[7]

- More than 90 percent of American Christians will never lead anyone to Christ,[8]

- More than 50 percent of our churches in America will lead no one at all to Christ this year. Not one person.[9]

Churches will raise a budget, conduct worship services on Sunday, have a wonderful choir, lead Sunday school, and do all the "churchy" stuff, but no one will come to Christ. We know more, we have more, and, yet, we seem to be doing less when it comes to fulfilling the first and last commandments of our Lord and Savior Jesus Christ.

First Jesus commanded, *"Follow me, and I will make you fishers of men."*[10] Last, He said, *"Go into all the world and preach the gospel to every creature."*[11]

How are we doing on these two commands?

There are roughly 7.5 billion people on earth today.[12] By most estimates, there are between 800 million and 1.1 billion evangelical Christians. That leaves over six billion that are lost. It remains a great tragedy that they have never heard the Gospel—many are within our own nation. It is no wonder we have so many crazy things going on here. When people don't know Jesus, and they're not filled with the Holy Spirit, they do the craziest things. It is amazing that we in the Church would expect anything else. Do you want to see them and their actions change? Someone must go tell them about Jesus. What is crazy is that we would expect them to change without our telling them about Jesus.

Light Always Wins

There is a wonderful book that I would highly recommend called *Surprising Insights from the Unchurched* by Thom Rainer. Thom is the President and CEO of Lifeway Christian Resources (of the Southern Baptist denomination) and is the former dean of the Billy Graham School of Missions, Evangelism, and Church Growth. This book presents an outstanding study of a number of folks who used to be unchurched and are now in church. While they could still remember being unchurched, Thom asked them a whole series of questions about what happened, what changed, and how it happened.

One of the surprising insights he had was the imperative of personal evangelism on the part of every Christian. Seventy-five percent of the formerly unchurched told him that someone from the church they joined came out and intentionally shared Christ with them.

One pastor from Louisiana stated bluntly, "You probably won't quote me on this, but I think most church leaders are basically stupid about reaching the unchurched. You know what they need to do? Tell lost people about Jesus; witness to them. I mean, what kind of crazy person expects to reach lost people without telling them about Jesus?"

Without an intentional, organized effort to share the Gospel with non-Christians, most lasting efforts to reach the unchurched will be in vain. The comments of Earl from Tampa, Florida, are instructive: "I thank God that my church sent people out to share Jesus with me. I thank God that they were trained how to share the Gospel with me. I thank God they loved me enough to be obedient to the Lord."[13]

William J. Bennett said, "In many parts of America we have become the kind of place to which civilized countries used to send missionaries."[14]

Disengaged Christians

Where is our passion in all of this? If our wallets tell the story, we should be concerned. Bob Sjogren reports in his book, *Unveiled at Last*, that 93 percent of every dollar given in the United States goes to services to ourselves; 6.9 percent goes to reach places that have already been reached; and only 1 tenth of 1 percent goes to reach the unreached with the Gospel.[15]

Could we be any more disengaged? And the problem is this: When we as Christians disengage and refuse to be salt and light to our generation, we dramatically impact our society for the negative.

Our nation's moral compass has gone haywire. We've bought into the theology of consumerism and the philosophy that you only go around once—grab all the gusto you can. Nothing really matters, so anything goes.

For the most part, we as Christians are not out there teaching God's rules, so any rule must be man's and, therefore, is arbitrary. Many people feel that rules just don't apply to them, or that they can be bent to suit their needs.

A survey conducted by the Josephson Institute of Ethics showed:

- 91 percent of Americans admit to lying regularly to people closest to them

- 74 percent steal items when they think they won't be missed

- 56 percent say they will drink and drive if they think they can handle it

- 55 percent say they would cheat on their spouse

- 40 percent confess to using illegal drugs

- 30 percent claim they cheat on their taxes

- 93 percent of adults and teens say that they and nobody else determine what is and isn't moral in their lives.[16]

When we disengage, all kinds of bad things happen. In only one day in America:

- 3,000 women will have an abortion and 3,445 un-married women will give birth to a child

- there will be 3,110 divorces

- 84 people will commit suicide and 45 people will die of AIDS

- 9,260 teenagers will have sex for the first time

- 28,206 people will be arrested; 4,274 of them for drug violations

- 3,396 households will declare bankruptcy

- 411 Americans will convert to the Muslim faith; 872 will become Mormons

- 8 churches will close their doors for the last time.[17]

And the crazy thing is that we disengage mostly because we don't think people want to hear what we have to say about Jesus. Although we don't always believe it, people are open to the Gospel.

Thirty Percent Accept Christ

At Evangelism Explosion, we conduct leadership-training clinics in the U. S. and around the world, and we take people out every week witnessing for Jesus. Nationwide, we see about 30 percent of those with whom we share the Gospel accept Christ.

People are amazingly open. One day my son Josh and I went with a group to a rather poor neighborhood to share the Gospel. We had hotdogs and sodas, some kids performed a few skits, and we heard someone give a testimony. Then we got to talk one-on-one with some of the folks who came out. We spoke with a man named Jerry. Jerry was 81 years old, and he was thrilled to hear about and accept Jesus. Right before we left he said, "I've been in this neighborhood for 51 years, and you all are the first Christians I remember seeing."

For the most part, we are just not out there. Instead, we live in silent rebellion to Jesus and His commands. When we disengage and become separatists, our society is negatively impacted and lost people lose. More than 2,000 people die every day here in the U.S. and go to an eternity in Hell separated from God.

Why do we allow this to happen?

I have thought a lot about this, and I'm sure I don't know the whole answer, but surely part of it must be that:

1. We have bought into false views of salvation like universalism (the belief that everyone is saved), auto-soteriology (the idea that we are saved by our own works), or perhaps we think that we are saved by membership in a particular church, or just by being religious.

2. It is possible that we don't understand our condition or the condition of those that are lost. We are confused over Heaven and Hell and we are poor judges of our condition. Over 70 percent of Americans viewed their chances of getting into Heaven as good or better.[18] The truth is that no one is saved without Jesus.

3. We don't understand our obligation before God to achieve His purposes in our lives. We have gotten it into our heads that we are our own. The Bible teaches us that we are not our own; we have been bought with a price. We are stewards of this life and sent by our master to take His light to everyone. We have forgotten Luke 15 and the parables of the lost sheep, lost coin, and the lost son. Here we see the intensity and passion of God for the lost.

4. Perhaps we imagine that we ourselves are too small to make a difference.

Here's the key question: **If we engage again, can America be reclaimed?** I believe, **YES**; America can and must be reclaimed for Christ, and we can be part of its happening during this generation.

Spiritual Multiplication

The reality is that if only one Christian were to share his or her faith with a non-believer, see that person come to saving faith in Jesus, and then teach them as well how to witness, within 34 generations of this process, everyone on earth would be reached.

Or, let's look at it another way: If every Christian would learn how to witness, start to pray that God would lead them to one person who would be open to the Gospel, share their faith and see them come to Christ, the Church would double in a very short period of time. If the person they won did the same and this process were repeated 4 times, the job would be done; Jesus would come again, and we could go home. Sound good to you?

The truth is, it is not only not impossible, it is relatively easy—if we would only be salt and light, get engaged, learn to share our faith, and get out there.

This is a process called Spiritual Multiplication, and it's powerful. Some have started to talk about it recently, but Dr. Kennedy talked about it for 47 years. Spiritual Multiplication is the answer from Holy Scripture for reaching our world for Christ.

It is an awesome responsibility to own a Bible. For the Bible is clear about our responsibility before Almighty God. We have been given two mandates, both tied together, inseparable: the Cultural Mandate to be "salt" and the Evangelism Mandate to be "light."

If we will only do what God has placed us here to do, we can shine like the stars forever, according to Daniel. Are you up to it? Maybe you say, "I'm not great enough for such heights." As Admiral William Halsey said, "There aren't any great men. There are just great challenges that ordinary men like you and me are forced by circumstances to meet."[19]

The great challenge and purpose of our lives must be to see this great nation and our world reached for Christ, and to see it transformed for the glory of God. It must become unacceptable to us that there are people alive who have never heard of Jesus. We must be both "salt" and "light."

- The heartbeat of the Church must be evangelism.

- All Christians are mandated to share their faith.

- The world is primed and ready for evangelism.

- Equipping and empowering laypeople is the key to

reaching the world for Christ.

Moreover, we know the outcome. The bottom line is: We win. I have read the last chapter of the Book. We win!

It is not hard for light to defeat darkness. Even if a room were pitch black, absolutely dark, without a ray of light coming in, it would only take a small candle to offer light to the very corners of the room.

Know this: we, by God's grace, will continue to lift high the standard for Christ and the Gospel in this nation because religious liberty for all is at stake. If that first liberty is lost, all other liberties will soon follow. It is our prayer that more and more Americans will grasp hold of our God-given rights and the rights given to us in our Constitution to determine our political destiny and preserve liberty for ourselves, our families, and this republic.

A Shining City on a Hill

As believers in Jesus Christ, we are called to send light into the darkness, wherever we are. It sure is a lot easier to send light and share the Gospel when you have the freedom to do so. As I say, much is at stake. The Gospel has gone forth from these shores. What nation has sent more missionaries? What nation has funded more missionary endeavors? Even today the United States is still the number one country for sending missionaries around the world.[20] It is the Gospel of Jesus Christ that makes the difference in the lives of men and women; and it is men and women who are compelled by that Gospel to live out their faith, who will make a difference as Christians in government office in our nation. That can make America a "shining city on a hill" once more.

That is why, if you and I truly want to see America changed and redeemed, we must pray—pray that people will be changed by the Gospel of Jesus Christ, so that as individuals are changed, whole communities, cities, and our nation will be changed. We certainly must vote in a way that expands our ability to carry out Christ's mission here on earth, and we must be engaged in the political process—and that includes running for elective office. Perhaps some of you reading this book should be running for Congress.

The bottom line is this: We must understand that real enduring change only comes as the human heart is transformed, and inner transformation is only made possible by faith in Jesus Christ. When the Gospel changes hearts and minds, then everything begins to change, and the same is as true for Washington D.C., as it is for the rest of America. That is the hope we have for America. This is why Dr. Kennedy remained optimistic about America to his very last breath. He believed that one day a generation of Christian men and women would rise up and take up this mission, and the ills of our society would disappear like the dew before a rising sun.

May we be that generation. May we be that people. Perhaps we have been born for such a time as this. May God grant us the ability to believe, and the courage to stand up and act, and may God bless you as you do.

CHAPTER 2

Freedom's Holy Light*

by Peter A. Lillback

For everything there is a season, and a time for every matter under heaven . . . a time for war, and a time for peace.
ECCLESIASTES 3:1, 8

Have you ever wondered why Congress opens its sessions in prayer? The reason is traceable to the Pilgrims' faith in Providence, which was continued by the men that gathered a century and a half later at the first Continental Congress in 1774. The history of the first prayer in Congress reveals our founding Patriots' commitment to Divine Providence, the integration point of faith and government.

Prayer: The First Act of Congress

America's first step toward independence began in Philadelphia in Carpenter's Hall. The Congress' first official act was to open in prayer. This was not a simple decision, however, and engendered great debate.[1] It was finally agreed that the first man to pray on behalf of the Congress would be Dr. Jacob Duché. His prayer in Carpenter's Hall, Philadelphia given at the first meeting of the First Continental Congress in September, 1774, says:

Our Lord, our Heavenly Father, high and mighty King of Kings, Lord of Lords, who dost from thy throne behold all the dwellers upon the earth, and **reignest with power supreme and uncontrolled over all kingdoms, empires, and governments**, look down in mercy, we beseech Thee, upon these American States who have fled to Thee from the rod of the Oppressor, **and thrown themselves upon Thy gracious protection**, desiring to be henceforth dependent only upon Thee.

To Thee have they appealed for the righteousness of their cause. To Thee do they now look up for that countenance and support which Thou alone canst give. Take them, therefore, Heavenly Father, under Thy nurturing care. Give them wisdom in council and valor in the field. Defeat the malicious design of our cruel adversaries. Convince them of the unrighteousness of their cause, and if they still persist in their sanguinary purpose, O let the voice of Thine own unerring justice, sounding in their hearts, constrain them to drop their weapons of war from their unnerved hands in the day of battle. Be Thou present, O Lord of Wisdom, and direct the Council of the honorable Assembly. Enable them to settle things upon the best and surest foundation, that the scene of blood may speedily be closed; that order, harmony, and peace may effectually be restored, and truth and justice, religion and piety, prevail and flourish amongst Thy people. Preserve the health of their bodies, the vigor of their minds. Shower down upon them, and the millions they here represent, such temporal blessings as Thou seest expedient for them in this world and crown them with everlasting glory in the world to come. All this we ask in the name and through the merits of Jesus Christ, Thy Son, our Savior. Amen.[2] [Emphasis is added, as it is throughout this chapter.]

In 1875, the Library of Congress produced a placard that summarized various reports from the founders on the impact that this first prayer had on the Continental Congress. It reads:

Washington was kneeling there, and Henry, Randolph, Rutledge, Lee, and Jay, and by their side there stood, bowed in reverence, the Puritan Patriots of New England, who at that moment had reason to believe that an armed soldiery was wasting their humble households. It was believed that Boston had been bombarded and destroyed . . . They prayed fervently "for America, for Congress, for the Province of Massachusetts Bay, and especially for the town of Boston," and who can realize the emotion with which **they turned imploringly to Heaven for Divine interposition and**—"It was enough" says Mr. Adams, "to melt a heart of stone. I saw the tears gush into the eyes of the old, grave, Pacific Quakers of Philadelphia."[3]

Patrick Henry, Revolutionary from Virginia, an Impassioned Patriot for Liberty

Patrick Henry's famous line, "Give me liberty, or give me death" is rarely given in its context. When that context is read, it is clear that Henry, like the other founders, had a deeply patriotic trust in Divine Providence. Henry spoke his immortal words in Richmond, Virginia on March 23, 1775. His stirring declaration reveals the founders' firm confidence in God's providential care for America:

There is no longer any room for hope. If we wish to be free...we must fight!—I repeat it, sir, we must fight! **An appeal to arms and to the God of Hosts is all that is left us**! . . . Three millions of people, armed in the holy cause of liberty . . . are invincible by any force which our enemy can send against us. Besides sir, we shall not fight our battles alone. **There is a just God who presides over the destinies of nations; and He will raise up friends to fight our battles for us**. The battle sir, is not to the strong alone; it is to the vigilant, the active, the brave . . . There is no retreat but in submission and slavery! . . . Gentlemen may cry, Peace! peace!—but there is no peace . . . Is life so dear, and peace so sweet, as to be purchased at the price of chains and slavery? Forbid it, Almighty God! I know not what course others may take; but as for me, give me liberty or give me death![4]

Days of Prayer and Fasting

The importance of Divine Providence was proclaimed to the new nation by the Continental Congress in its repeated calls for days of prayer and fasting. In March 1776, for example, the Congress declared:

It becomes the indispensable duty of these hitherto free and happy colonies, with true penitence of heart, and the most reverent devotion, **publickly to acknowledge the over ruling Providence of God**; to confess and deplore our offences against him; and to supplicate his interposition for averting the threatened danger, and prospering our strenuous efforts in the cause of freedom, virtue, and posterity. . . . Do earnestly recommend, that Friday, the Seventeenth day of May next, be observed by the said colonies as a day of humiliation, fasting, and prayer; that we may, with united hearts, confess and bewail our manifold sins and transgressions, and, by a sincere repentance and amendment of life, appease his righteous displeasure, and through the merits and mediation of Jesus Christ, obtain his pardon and forgiveness. . . . That he would be graciously pleased to bless all his people in these colonies with health and plenty, and grant that a spirit of incorruptible patriotism, and of pure undefiled religion, may universally prevail; and this continent be speedily restored to the blessings of peace and liberty, and enabled to transmit them inviolate to the latest posterity. And it is recommended to Christians of all denominations, to assemble for public worship, and abstain from servile labour on the said day.[5]

Days of Thanksgiving

The Congress also called for a day of thanksgiving on October 18, 1780, in the wake of the failed plot by Benedict Arnold to betray the American cause into the hands of the British:

Whereas it **hath pleased Almighty God, the Father of all mercies amidst the vicissitudes and calamities of war, to bestow blessings on the people of these states,** which call for their devout and thankful acknowledgements, more especially in the late remarkable interposition of his watchful providence in the rescuing the person of our Commander-in-Chief and the army from imminent dangers, at the moment when treason was ripened for execution. . . . It is therefore recommended to the several states . . . a day of public thanksgiving and prayer, that all the people may assemble on that **day to celebrate the praises of our Divine Benefactor**; to confess our unworthiness of the least of his favours, and to offer our fervent supplications to the God of all grace . . . to cause the knowledge of Christianity to spread over all the earth.

Many other examples of the founders' trust in God can be discovered in their Thanksgiving and Prayer and Fasting Proclamations preserved in the records of the *Journals of the Continental Congress*.[6]

The Peace Treaty with Great Britain

When peace was finally won with Great Britain at the end of the Revolutionary War, the Treaty signed by the Continental Congress in 1783 affirmed the role of Providence in bringing hostility to an end:

> **In the name of the Most Holy and Undivided Trinity**. It having pleased the Divine Providence to dispose the hearts of the most serene and most potent Prince George the Third, by the Grace of God, King of Great Britain. . . . and of the United States of America, to forget all past misunderstandings and differences . . .[7]

Great Britain had an established Church, but The United States of America did not. Both, however, recognized that the rule of Divine Providence was the transcendent point where faith and government necessarily connected.

George Washington, the Preacher of Divine Providence

George Washington was placed on the one-dollar bill for good reason. He was the champion of the Revolutionary War, and more. He was already being called "the father of his country" during his lifetime. At his funeral, he was eulogized as "first in war, first in peace, and first in the hearts of his countrymen." As the hero of the nation, his views were especially important. His deep commitment to the providence of God is, thus, particularly significant.

Washington's earliest dramatic experience of God's providential protection occurred during General Braddock's defeat at the Battle of the Monongahela, near modern day Pittsburgh, in 1755. Following the Battle, Washington wrote to his brother, John A. Washington on July 18, 1755:

> But **by the all-powerful dispensations of Providence, I have been protected beyond all human probability or expectation**; for I had four bullets through my coat, and two horses shot under me, yet escaped unhurt, although death was leveling my companions on every side of me.

This remarkable story prompted the colonial Presbyterian preacher Rev. Samuel Davies of Hanover, Virginia, and later president of the College at Princeton, N. J., to declare in a sermon entitled "Religion and Patriotism: The Constituents of a Good Soldier," "I cannot but hope **Providence has hitherto preserved him in so signal a manner**, for some important service to his country." Moreover, Washington's grandson relates an astounding story of a subsequent encounter by Washington sixteen years later in 1770 with some of the very Indians who had sought to kill him at Braddock's defeat.[8]

General Washington, Military Leader

Twenty years after Washington's experience of "the all-powerful dispensations of Providence" at Monongahela, he would be selected as the General of the Continental Army. The leaders of the new nation committed their military commander to the protection of Divine Providence. Thus, on July 13, 1775, Governor Jonathan Trumbull of Connecticut, who would become known as "Brother Jonathan" for his faithful support of General Washington all through the War, wrote to the General:

> The Honorable Congress have proclaimed a Fast to be observed by the inhabitants of all the English Colonies on this continent, to stand before the Lord in one day, with public humiliation, fasting and prayer, to deplore our many sins, to offer up our joint supplications to God, for forgiveness, and for his merciful interposition for us in this day of unnatural darkness and distress... They have, with one united voice, appointed you to the high station you possess. **The Supreme Director of all events hath caused a wonderful union of hearts and counsels to subsist among us.** Now therefore, be strong and very courageous . . . **May the God of the armies of Israel shower down the blessing of his Divine Providence on you,** give you wisdom and fortitude, cover your head in the day of battle and danger, add success, convince our enemies of their mistaken measures, and that all their attempts to deprive these Colonies of their inestimable constitutional rights and liberties are injurious and vain.

Consistent with Washington's early experience of God's providential aid at the battle of Monongahela are his remarks penned on August 20, 1778, as the commander in chief of the Revolutionary Army. Referring to recent instances of divine intervention during the War for Independence, Washington wrote to Brigadier-General Nelson, describing himself as a man of faith and as a preacher of Providence.

> **The hand of Providence has been conspicuous in all this, that he must be worse than an infidel that lacks faith,** and more than wicked that has not

gratitude enough to acknowledge his obligations. But it will be time enough for me to turn preacher when my present appointment ceases; and therefore, I shall add no more on the doctrine of Providence.

Frequently throughout his career, Washington asserted the reality of Divine Providence. On the first of May, 1777, the American camp learned that France was joining the war on the side of America. Announcing this most significant French decision to his Army, Washington proclaimed at Valley Forge:

> **It having pleased the Almighty Ruler of the universe to defend the cause of the United American States**, and finally to raise up a powerful friend among the princes of the earth, to establish our liberty and independence upon a lasting foundation, it becomes us to set apart a day for gratefully acknowledging the divine goodness, and celebrating the important event, which **we owe to His divine interposition.**

On October 20th in 1781, General Washington called for a service to give thanks for the British surrender at Yorktown the day before:

> The commander in chief earnestly recommends that the troops not on duty should universally attend with that seriousness of deportment and gratitude of heart which the **recognition of such reiterated and astonishing interposition of Providence** demands of us.

President Washington, Servant Leader

Washington's opportunity to become a preacher of Providence occurred at his Inauguration as the first President of the United

States under the American Constitution. A portion of Washington's *First Inaugural Address*, delivered April 30, 1789, is as follows:

> It would be peculiarly improper to omit, in this first official act, my fervent **supplications to that Almighty Being who rules over the universe**, [and] who presides in the councils of nations, and whose providential aids can supply every human defect, that His benediction may consecrate to the liberties and happiness of the people of the United States.

On October 3rd in 1789, mindful of the many blessings God had bestowed upon America, President Washington proclaimed a Day of Thanksgiving:

> **It is the duty of all nations to acknowledge the Providence of Almighty God**, to obey His will, to be grateful for His benefits, and humbly to implore His protection and favor.

Washington, who assured the synagogue in New Port, Rhode Island, that the American government ". . . gives to bigotry no sanction, to persecution no assistance,"[9] also saw the duty of America to acknowledge and adore the care of Divine Providence for the American people. In his First Inaugural Address (April 30, 1789), he declared,

> No people can be bound to **acknowledge and adore the Invisible Hand** which conducts the affairs of men more than the people of the United States. Every step by which they have advanced to the character of an independent nation seems to have been distinguished by some token of providential agency . . . We ought to be no less persuaded that the

propitious smiles of Heaven can never be expected on a nation that disregards the eternal rules of order and right which Heaven itself has ordained.

The Constitution—the "Miracle" of Divine Providence

General Washington was selected to preside over the Constitutional Convention. He set the tone of the gathering soon after his arrival in Philadelphia:

> If to please the people we offer what we ourselves disapprove, how can we afterwards defend our work? Let us raise a standard to which the wise and the honest can repair; the event is in the hands of God.

Looking back at the Constitutional Convention from the vantage point of the following summer, Washington saw God's intervention in the production of the American Constitution. On June 30, 1788, after the ratification of the Constitution, Washington wrote to Benjamin Lincoln:

> No Country upon Earth ever had it more in its power to attain these blessings . . . Much to be regretted indeed would it be, were we to neglect the means and depart from the **road which Providence has pointed us to**, so plainly; I cannot believe it will ever come to pass. **The Great Governor of the Universe has led us too long and too far** . . . to forsake us in the midst of it . . . We may, now and then, get bewildered; but I hope and trust that there is good sense and virtue enough left to recover the right path.

Consider also, Washington's letter to his good friend, Governor

Jonathan Trumbull of Connecticut. General Washington wrote on
July 20, 1788:

> We may, with a kind of grateful and pious exultation,
> trace **the finger of Providence** through those dark
> and mysterious events, which first induced the States
> to appoint a general Convention and then led them
> one after another into an adoption of the system
> recommended by that general Convention; thereby
> in all human probability, laying a lasting foundation
> for tranquility and happiness.

In fact, Washington wrote to his dear French friend and fellow
warrior Marquis de Lafayette calling the Constitution a "miracle."[10]
James Madison also considered the Constitution to be the result of a
miracle. In a letter to Jefferson he says, "It is impossible to consider the
degree of concord which ultimately prevailed as less than a miracle."[11]

During the convention, Alexander Hamilton said the following,
as reported and summarized by Madison:

> This was the critical moment for forming such a
> Government. We should run every risk in trusting
> to future amendments. As yet we retain the habits
> of union. We are weak & sensible of our weakness.
> Henceforward the motives will become feebler, and
> the difficulties greater. **It is a miracle** that we are
> now here exercising our tranquil & free deliberations
> on the subject. It would be madness to trust to
> future miracles. A thousand causes must obstruct a
> reproduction of them.[12]

It is time for our great nation to remember that we are indeed
one nation under God. The God of Providence proclaimed by the

Church is also the God of Providence who must be recognized as the "wise and loving Creator" and sustainer of our Nation. And so, it is good that our nation is rediscovering the power of faith-based organizations. People of faith have had significant success in changing hardened hearts of crime. Recognizing this success, both Republican and Democratic candidates have publicly championed faith-based approaches to address the social ills of our nation. We need not be fearful of this cooperative labor of government and church, for in America's heritage, faith and government are not antithetical.

Indeed, President Washington emphasized the necessity of religion and morality for our constitutional government. In his Farewell Address written over two hundred years ago on September 17, 1796, he declared the following; and with this we close this quick survey of Providence and the founding of America:

> **Of all the dispositions and habits which lead to political prosperity, Religion and Morality are indispensable supports.** In vain would that man claim the tribute of Patriotism, who should labor to subvert these great pillars of human happiness, these firmest props of the duties of Men and Citizens. The mere Politician, equally with the pious man, ought to respect and to cherish them. A volume could not trace all their connections with private and public felicity . . . And let us with caution indulge the supposition that morality can be maintained without religion. Whatever may be conceded to the influence of refined education on minds of peculiar structure, **reason and experience both forbid us to expect that national morality can prevail in exclusion of religious principle.**

* This essay is a chapter in Dr. Lillback's book, *Freedom's Holy Light: "With A Firm Reliance On Divine Providence."*

CHAPTER 3

The Genius of the United States Constitution

by John Hostettler

. . . for all have sinned and fall short of the glory of God . . .
ROMANS 3:23

The Constitution for the United States of America has been called the greatest work ever penned by uninspired men. This is an allusion to the greatest work ever penned by *inspired* men—the Bible. But the genius of the United States Constitution can only truly be understood in light of its framers' understanding of one of the most fundamental precepts of Holy Writ—the fallen nature of man.

Shortly after the Federal Convention of 1787 concluded and the delegates returned home to begin the arduous process of convincing their fellow citizens in their respective states to ratify the "plan of the Convention,"[1] Alexander Hamilton, John Jay, and James Madison embarked on a writing campaign to convince the people of the state of New York to adopt the Constitution. In a series of submissions to a select number of newspapers in the state, the three giants of our political ancestry penned various essays explaining and extolling the merits of the work of the delegates. Though Jay was not a delegate to the convention, New York delegate Alexander Hamilton solicited his esteemed fellow New Yorker to help in this effort. Hamilton also employed the aid of fellow delegate from Virginia, James Madison, to lend his influence in pressing the cause in New York. Ultimately the series of essays was compiled and published as a part of the works of James Madison, and we know them today as "The Federalist" or "The Federalist Papers." The Library of Congress describes this collection as "the most significant American contribution to political thought."[2] It can, therefore, be asserted with some force that James Madison's explanation of the justification and purpose, generally speaking, of government found in Federalist Paper No. 51 may be the "most significant American" ideal regarding the very idea of government.

Many of us are familiar with the first part of Madison's explanation because it fits a popular and idealistic narrative, which suggests that the Constitution—the plan of the Federal Convention of 1787—was framed in order to preserve liberty. But this narrative confuses a result with a reason or, once again, a justification for the government constructed by the framers. To clear up this confusion, let's hear from Mr. Madison. And let's hear everything that he had to say. James Madison wrote:

> But what is **government** itself, but **the greatest of all reflections on human nature?** If men were angels, no government would be necessary. If angels were to govern men, neither external nor internal controls on government would be necessary. **In framing a government** which is to be administered by men over men, the great difficulty lies in this: **you must first enable the government to control the governed** [i.e. "We the People"]; and in the next place oblige it to control itself.[3] [Emphasis is added, as it is throughout this chapter.]

Therefore, the Constitution reflects a realistic view of fallen humanity. First, the Constitution was necessary in order to grant the government the requisite authority to control the governed; i.e., "men" and not "angels." Second, the Constitution was framed in such a way that the government—*manned* by "men" and not "angels"— would implicitly control itself as a result of the limited authority with which it was *constituted* to exercise.

A Convention Is Called

Put another way, a convention to revise the Articles of Confederation was called, in large part, because the Articles had effectively failed to convince the legislatures of thirteen free and independent states to consistently perform two functions fundamentally important to the survival of any political union— supply revenue and troops to the federal government. In Federalist Paper No. 23 Alexander Hamilton explained the motivation of the Convention's delegates this way:

> Defective as the present [Articles of] Confederation [have] been proved to be . . . It was presumed [by the Articles' framers] that a sense of [the states'] true interests, and a regard to the dictates of good faith, would be found sufficient pledges for the punctual performance of the duty of the members [i.e. the states] to the federal head.

> The experiment has, however, demonstrated that this expectation was ill-founded and illusory . . . The result from all this is that the Union ought to be invested with full power to levy troops; to build and equip fleets; and to raise the revenues which will be required for the formation and support of an army and navy, in the customary and ordinary modes

practiced in other governments.[4]

Note that Hamilton described a presumption on the part of
the framers of the Articles of Confederation that "a sense of true
interests, a regard to the dictates of good faith, would be sufficient"
inspiration for the states to promptly meet their obligations to the
Union. However, this nearly utopian perspective of human nature
proved to be "ill-founded and illusory." Why? Because man does
not naturally operate by the "dictates of good faith"—even if it is
consistent with his "true interests" and those of his fellow citizens to
do so.

Therefore, it became evident that a new government must be
created. In fact, Hamilton argued in the same Federalist Paper that
there was "an absolute necessity for an entire change in the first
principles of the system" adopted under the Articles of Confederation.
He continued by proclaiming to his fellow New Yorkers that "if we
are in earnest about giving the Union energy and duration . . . we
must extend the laws of the federal government to the individual
citizens of America." Once again, it would be those laws of the federal
government—enacted by a legislative Congress—which would be
extended, by way of a newly fashioned executive authority, directly
to the individual citizens of America. Finally, "the laws of the federal
government" would "enable the government to control the governed."

The Genius of the Framers

So how is the genius of the Constitution's framers reflected in their
work product? How does the Constitution accomplish the seemingly
impossible tasks of simultaneously "enabl[ing] the government to
control the governed" and "oblig[ing] it to control itself?" We will
answer these questions by examining one of the most controversial
issues of the day—"paper money."

At the Federal Convention of 1787, delegates wrestled with an issue
that had plagued the states since the end of the war with Great Britain.

South Carolina delegate Charles Cotesworth Pinckney declared, "A majority of the people in South Carolina were **notoriously** for paper money as a legal tender."[5] Elbridge Gerry of Massachusetts said of his constituents, "They are for paper money when the Legislatures are against it. In Massachusetts, the County Conventions had declared a wish for a **depreciating paper** that would **sink itself**."[6] Connecticut's Roger Sherman succinctly summarized the sentiment of the Convention when he announced that the collective experience of the states had resulted in "a favorable crisis for crushing paper money."[7]

In response to this "crisis," the delegates included provisions in Article I, Section 10 which not only prohibited the states from coining money but also from issuing paper money. The paper money prohibition declares, "No State shall . . . emit Bills of Credit." A "bill of credit" was essentially a note issued by a state government that was intended to circulate as money and was redeemable against the state treasury, ostensibly for gold and silver coin. The widespread abuse of this system had resulted in the "crisis" mentioned by Connecticut delegate Roger Sherman.

So it happened that the Convention's delegates had observed a "crisis" resulting from the lack of government control on their fallen fellow citizens. It was the Constitution that "crushed" this mechanism of depravity. Once again, this law of the federal government—namely the Constitution—"enable[d] the government to control the governed" by denying the governed the use of state-issued paper money.

But if the Constitution was used for the "crushing" of paper money on the state level, wasn't there a need to do so on the federal level as well? The same "governed" who were obviously not "angels" in their financial affairs relative to the state authority, would not transform into angels with regard to a newly framed federal authority, would they? Obviously not. Additionally, there would be the problem of a new federal authority that might eventually command an uncontrollable level of power, given the necessary supremacy of the federal government relative to the authority of the states, regarding the power of making and regulating money. Therefore, not only were the framers effectively charged to control the governed by "crushing paper money" on the federal level, they also had to find a way of obliging the federal government to control itself in matters related to a sound monetary system for the Union.

To be sure, there was no desire to remove a crisis from the respective states and perpetuate it on the federal level. The Union had already suffered as a result of the explicit introduction of a fatal flaw in its earliest plan of governance. Article IX of the Articles of Confederation provided that "the United States, in congress assembled, shall have authority . . . to borrow money or **emit bills** on the **credit** of the United States."

Not long into the Constitutional Convention's proceedings, Virginia delegate Edmund Randolph highlighted the fact that the drafters of the Articles of Confederation had not foreseen "the havoc of paper money,"[8] which would ultimately pervade a Union less perfect than that which he and his fellow delegates felt a moral imperative to propose. This situation led Randolph's fellow Virginian James Madison to suggest in Federalist Paper No. 10 that a more perfect Union would be one in which "a **rage for paper money**, for an abolition of debts, for an equal division of property, or for any other improper or wicked project, [would] be less apt to pervade" that Union.[9]

Note that a concept—"paper money"—explicitly provided for in the Articles of Confederation had become uniformly regarded as a "wicked project" between the time of its introduction into that governing document and the time of the Federal Convention of 1787. It's hard to believe that the drafters of those original Articles— penned less than seventeen months after adoption of the Declaration of Independence—considered their work in any other way than on the side of the "angels."

The Federalist Paper writers reserved such moral outrage for a select few—very few—topics. In fact, only one such concept was actually explicitly sanctioned by a select few who had nobly striven for the blessings of liberty against overwhelming odds just a few years prior to the Constitutional Convention. So how would the Convention's delegates guarantee—as much as any generation can guarantee anything for their posterity—that such a "wicked project" would not again rear its ugly head and extinguish the blessings of liberty by, in this specific case, laying waste to the monetary system of the Union? As it happens, Madison actually answered that question in the same Federalist Paper by describing the *legal* status of the "project" of "paper money" in close proximity to his *moral* characterization of the same "project." The Constitution's framers obliged the revised federal government to control itself by rendering the "wicked project" of "paper money" likewise "improper."

The Federal Government Is Obliged to Control Itself

The means by which the Constitution's framers transformed a provision of the Articles of Confederation into one that was "improper" under the Constitution reveals how the delegates "oblige[d] the federal government] to control itself." The delegates to the Federal Convention of 1787 did not repeat the mistake made by those men who fashioned the Articles of Confederation in 1777. The delegates to the Federal Convention of 1787 did not *constitute* a federal government with the authority to "**emit bills** on the **credit** of the United States" as did the delegates who fashioned the Articles of Confederation in 1777. They simply left it out. This is the other half of the genius of the United States Constitution. It's the genius of any written constitution. A written constitution—such as the Constitution for the United States of America—means what it says, and it doesn't mean what it doesn't say. A written constitution obliges the government it constitutes to control itself by what it doesn't say.

Two icons of our political ancestry—two unsurpassed experts on Constitutional construction—explained this genius in two of the most seminal works on American polity. Their descriptions are two sides of the same coin—no pun intended.

After the Federalist President John Adams approved the Federalist-controlled Congress' "Alien and Sedition" Acts in 1798, Constitutional Convention delegate, Federalist Paper author, and former Congressman, Democratic Republican James Madison penned the Virginia Resolutions of 1798. In those resolutions, produced for the state legislature of Virginia, Madison objected to the enactment of the Alien and Sedition Acts by saying, in part, the following:

> . . . the General Assembly doth particularly protest against the palpable and alarming **infractions of the [U.S.] constitution**, in the two late cases of the "alien and sedition acts," passed at the last session of Congress; **the first of which exercises a power no where delegated to the federal government**; and which by uniting legislative and judicial powers, to those of executive, subverts the general principles of free government, as well as the particular organization and positive provisions of the federal constitution: and **the other of which acts, exercises in like manner a power not delegated by the constitution**, . . .[10]

In this statement of principle, Madison characterizes powers "not delegated by the constitution . . . to the federal government" as "infractions of the [U.S.] constitution." In other words, the Constitution was here violated by Congress's attempt to exercise authority where there is none *constituted*, or, for which there are no powers explicitly delegated regarding aliens and sedition. Hence, the government is obliged to control itself due to what the Constitution doesn't say.

In his *Commentaries on the Constitution of the United States,*

Supreme Court Justice and Harvard University Law Professor Joseph Story explained that infractions of the U.S. Constitution can be recognized not only because of what the Constitution doesn't say but because of what the Constitution does say. In explaining a particular rule of Constitutional construction, Story declared the following:

> This is one of the appropriate illustrations of the rule, that the affirmation of a power in particular cases, excludes it in all others . . . Affirmative words often, in their operation, imply a negative of other objects, than those affirmed; and in this case a negative, or exclusive sense, must be given to the words, or they have no operation at all.[11]

This "rule" described by Story provides that we can recognize infractions of the U.S. Constitution that occur when Congress attempts to exercise a power not "affirmed"—or explicitly delegated—in the Constitution. The federal government is obliged to limit itself to those powers "affirmed" and may not extend its authority beyond what is explicitly affirmed. Hence, the government is obliged to control itself due to what it does say.

Though space constraints limit our discussion of the framers' undeniable understanding of the fallen nature of man, they don't limit our realization of the source of that understanding. Which is why it *may* be said that the genius of the Constitution for the United States of America may, in fact, result from its status as the *second* most profound work ever penned by inspired men.

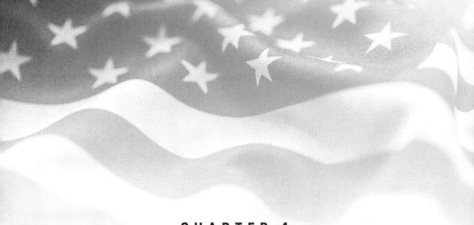

CHAPTER 4

A History of the Separation of Church and State

by William J. Federer

Jesus said to them, "Render to Caesar the things that are Caesar's, and to God the things that are God's." And they marveled at him.
MARK 12:17

On February 9, 1961, President John F. Kennedy addressed those gathered for the ninth annual prayer breakfast sponsored by the International Christian Leadership, Inc., a nondenominational group of laymen. In his remarks, President Kennedy acknowledged the foundation and heritage of America's religious freedom:

> This country was founded by men and women who were dedicated or came to be dedicated to two propositions: first, a strong religious conviction, and secondly, a recognition that this conviction could flourish only under a system of freedom. . . . The

Puritans and the Pilgrims of my own section of New England, the Quakers of Pennsylvania, the Catholics of Maryland, the Presbyterians of North Carolina, the Methodists and Baptists who came later, all shared these two great traditions which, like silver threads, have run through the warp and the woof of American History.

In order to understand the relationship between church and state in the American experience, it's needful to back up and look at what was happening in Europe after the Reformation.

Europe's Established Churches

After the Reformation, the Peace of Augsburg (1555) started a ripple effect across Europe, where, in the succeeding years, different kings chose different denominations of Christianity for their kingdoms. A partial list includes:

- ITALY, SPAIN, PORTUGAL, AUSTRIA, POLAND, LIECHTENSTEIN, LITHUANIA, LUXEMBOURG, MALTA, MONACO were Roman Catholic.

- HUNGARY was a majority Catholic with Calvinist, Lutheran, and Hungarian Byzantine-Catholic minorities.

- FRANCE established the Roman Catholic Church. Dissenters were Protestant Huguenots.

- IRELAND established the Church of Ireland (Anglican) till 1871. Dissenting Catholics made up a majority of the population, especially in the south.

- SWITZERLAND established the Calvinist Church in the eastern cantons and the Roman Catholic Church in the western cantons.

- GERMANY consisted of numerous kingdoms (Prussia, Saxony, Bavaria, etc.). The Lutheran Church was established in northern kingdoms. Dissenters included Anabaptists, called Mennonites and Amish.

- THE NETHERLANDS (Holland) established the Dutch Reformed Church with liberal toleration of dissenters in the north and the Roman Catholic Church in the south.

- BELGIUM established the Roman Catholic Church. Dissenters in the north were Anglicans and Protestants.

- SWEDEN established the Church of Sweden (Evangelical Lutheran).

- DENMARK established the Church of Denmark (Evangelical Lutheran).

- FINLAND established the Church of Finland (Evangelical Lutheran).

- NORWAY established the Church of Norway (Evangelical Lutheran).

- ICELAND established the Church of Iceland (Evangelical Lutheran).

- ROMANIA established the Romanian Orthodox Church.

- SERBIA established the Serbian Orthodox Church.

- CROATIA was mostly Roman Catholic and Croatian Greek Catholic.

- GREECE established the Greek Orthodox Church.

- RUSSIA established the Russian Orthodox Church.

- BULGARIA established the Bulgarian Orthodox Church.

- ARMENIA established the Armenian Apostolic Church.

- CYPRESS was mostly Cypriot Orthodox, with a Sunni Muslim minority.

- SCOTLAND established the Church of Scotland (Presbyterian).

- ENGLAND established the Church of England (Anglican). Dissenters were Puritans, Separatists, and Quakers.

In Europe during the 1500-1800s, only one denomination was allowed or preferred in each country. Whatever a king believed—his kingdom had to believe. If someone believed differently than their king, they were considered guilty of treason.

In the following centuries this resulted in wars, displaced peoples, and mass migrations across Europe, simply for conscience sake. A typical "established" church was supported by:

1. Mandatory attendance

2. Mandatory tithes

3. One could not hold public office unless they were a faithful member of the established denomination.

In most cases, church leaders were selected or approved by government leaders and paid salaries by the government. Dissenters, nonconformists, and Jews suffered disadvantages, were taxed, penalized, punished, persecuted, banished, or killed. Eventually, some of these displaced—mostly Christian refugees—spilled over and founded the colonies in America.

Meanwhile, when England's King Henry VIII broke away from the Roman Catholic Church so that he could divorce his wife with Church approval, he declared himself the head of the Church of England. Under his reign, translators were able to produce the Bible in English.

But something unexpected happened—people began to read it and compare the actions of King Henry to what was in the book. A movement arose to "purify" the Church of England. Members of the movement were nicknamed "Puritans." The King obviously did not think he or his church needed "purifying," so he persecuted them. A century later, England's King James I enforced religious conformity, stating he would "harry them out of the land."[1]

Another group gave up hope of trying to "purify" the Church of England. They were called "Separatists" because they met in secret, at night, by candlelight, in barns and basements, similar to illegal house churches in China or North Korea today. These Separatists were punished by being put in stocks, whipped, imprisoned, or even branded as heretics.

In 1607, a group of these Separatists who came to be called "Pilgrims," fled to Holland where they lived for twelve years. Seeing their children assimilating into the Dutch culture, they realized they would be a short-lived movement unless they did something—so they sailed to America in 1620.

At the Bicentennial Celebration of the landing of the Pilgrims at Plymouth Rock, Secretary of State Daniel Webster stated on December 22, 1820:

> There is a . . . sort of genius of the place, which . . . awes us. We feel that we are on the spot where the first scene of our history was laid; where the hearths and altars of New England were first placed; where Christianity, and civilization . . . made their first lodgement, in a vast extent of country . . . "If God prosper us," might have been the . . . language of our fathers, when they landed upon this Rock, ". . . we shall here begin a work which shall last for ages . . . We shall fill this region of the great continent . . . with civilization and Christianity.[2]

George Bancroft (1800–1891), who was Secretary of the Navy under President Polk, established the U.S. Naval Academy at Annapolis and the Naval Observatory in Washington, D.C. Bancroft wrote in *History of the United States* (1834–1876):

> Puritanism had exalted the laity . . . For him the wonderful counsels of the Almighty had appointed a Saviour; for him the laws of nature had been compelled and consulted, the heavens had opened, the earth had quaked, the sun had veiled his face, and Christ had died and risen again.[3]

Harvard Professor James Russell Lowell (1819–1891) was U.S. Minister to Spain and editor of the *Atlantic Monthly* and *North American Review*. In *Literary Essays* (1810–1890), he wrote "New England Two Centuries Ago." "Puritanism, believing itself quick with the seed of religious liberty, laid, without knowing it, the egg of democracy."[4]

Puritan Religious Uniformity Led to Other Settlements

After the Puritans settled Massachusetts, they extended religious toleration only to Puritans. Their fear was that if other denominations were tolerated, they might gain ascendancy and persecute Puritans again—a memory still fresh in their minds from England. Puritans had a kind of "us–versus–them" mentality. Though Puritans did not like the government controlling their churches in England, they favored it in America, as they were in charge of the government.

When Boston's Puritan leader, Rev. John Cotton, enforced religious conformity, dissenting pastors and their churches fled, founding new communities.

A generation before Europe's "Age of Enlightenment" and John Locke's *Two Treatises of Government* (1680-1690), Scotland's Presbyterian "Covenanters" championed the Old Testament model of Israel's covenant with God. This idea came to New England with pastors who founded communities:

- Rev. Thomas Hooker founded Hartford, Connecticut, in 1636;

- Rev. Roger Williams founded Providence, Rhode Island, in 1636;

- Rev. John Wheelwright founded Exeter, New Hampshire, in 1638;

- Rev. John Lothropp founded Barnstable, Massachusetts, in 1639.

Rev. Roger Williams Decries Christian Persecution

Roger Williams wrote *The Bloody Tenet [Practice] of Persecution for Conscience Sake* in 1644, stating:

> Mr. Cotton . . . hath not duly considered these following particulars . . . That the Church of the Jews under the Old Testament in the type and the Church of the Christians under the New Testament in the antitype, were both **separate** from the world; and that when they have opened a gap in the hedge, or **wall of separation**, between the garden of the Church and the wilderness of the world, God hath ever broken down the wall itself, removed the candlestick . . . and made his garden a wilderness, as at this day. And that therefore if He will ever please to restore His garden and paradise again, it must of necessity be walled in peculiarly unto Himself from the world, and that all that shall be saved out of the world are to be transplanted out of the wilderness of the world and added unto His Church or garden . . . a **separation** of Holy from unHoly, penitent from impenitent, Godly from unGodly."[5] [Emphasis added, as it is throughout this chapter..]

Rev. Roger Williams was alluding to the passage in Isaiah 5:1–7. When God's people sin, He judges them by allowing His vineyard to be trampled by an ungodly government:

> My well-beloved hath a vineyard . . . And he fenced it . . . and planted it with the choicest vine . . . and he looked that it should bring forth grapes, and it

brought forth wild grapes. And now, O inhabitants
of Jerusalem . . . judge, I pray you, betwixt me and my
vineyard. . . . when I looked that it should bring forth
grapes, brought it forth wild grapes? . . . I will tell
you what I will do to my vineyard: I will take away
the hedge thereof, and it shall be eaten up; and break
down **the wall** thereof, and it shall be trodden down
. . . For the vineyard . . . is the house of Israel . . . he
looked for judgment, but behold oppression.

Williams wrote in *Plea for Religious Liberty* (1644):

The God of Peace, the God of Truth will shortly
seal this truth, and confirm this witness, and make
it evident to the whole world, that the doctrine of
persecution for cause of conscience, is most evidently
and lamentably contrary to the doctrine of Christ
Jesus the Prince of Peace."[6]

As we will see later, Roger Williams' phrase of a "wall of separation" between church and state would be picked up almost two
centuries later by Thomas Jefferson

Colonial Charters and Established Denominations

Following the example of Europe, each colony initially favored
only one denomination, providing them, in many cases, with state
tax support, special privileges, and requiring mandatory church
membership of its citizens, and if a person did not believe the way
their colony's government did, they were persecuted and fled. The
attitude generally was "if you do not like our denomination, fine,
start your own colony." This caused rival denominations to leave and
start new settlements favoring their own denomination.

Virginia was established a Church of England, or Anglican

colony, which meant:

1. Mandatory membership in the Anglican Church;

2. Mandatory taxes to support the Anglican Church;

3. One could not hold office unless they took the oath of supremacy, acknowledging the king as the head of the Church.

4. Residents were required to attend church, as a Virginia ordinance stated, March 5, 1624: "Whosoever shall absent himself from Divine service any Sunday without an allowable excuse shall forfeit a pound of tobacco."

The original denominations in the Colonies were primarily Protestant.

NEW ENGLAND COLONIES:
- Massachusetts 1630 – Puritan
- Rhode Island 1636 – Baptist
- Connecticut 1636 – Congregational
- New Hampshire 1638 – Congregational

MIDDLE COLONIES:
- New York 1626 – Dutch Reformed
- Delaware 1638 – Lutheran & Dutch Reformed
- Pennsylvania 1682 – Quaker & Lutheran
- New Jersey 1664 – Lutheran & Dutch Reformed

SOUTHERN COLONIES:
- Virginia 1607 – Anglican

- Maryland 1633 – Catholic
- North Carolina 1653 – Anglican
- South Carolina 1663 – Anglican
- Georgia 1732 – Protestant

Though not part of the 13 Colonies at the time, there were also other settlements:

- Spanish Florida 1565 – Catholic
- French Canada & Louisiana Territory 1604 – Catholic

Over time, due to the sparse population in America, settlers found that by working together they would all mutually benefit economically. They bonded during times of distress such as famines, smallpox epidemics, Indian attacks, and wars.

When the War for Independence started, they all had to work together to be free from the King of England. After the American Revolution, their attitude became, "we may not agree on religion all the time, but you were willing to fight and die for my freedom, I need to let you practice yours."

Christians gradually convinced themselves to tolerate those with whom they did not agree because of:

1. Jesus' teaching to "do unto others as you would have them do unto you";

2. Jesus' example of never forcing anyone to follow Him;

3. Jesus' command to share the Gospel, thus, allowing non-Christians into their colonies in hopes of evangelizing them.

Time eventually brought an end to each coloney's mandatory tax support and special privileges for the state-sanctioned denominations.

Rather than viewing the many denominations as the Body of Christ tragically being divided, it was viewed positively—as a sort of free market competition for converts, insuring that no one denomination would become so large as to become the official denomination of the state, as was the case in European countries.

Charles Carroll, the only Catholic to sign the Declaration of Independence, wrote to Rev. John Stanford, October, 9, 1827:

> Observing the Christian religion divided into many sects, I founded the hope that no one would be so predominant as to become the religion of the state. That hope was thus early entertained because all of them joined in the same cause.

America gave birth to a new kind of liberty which would benefit all immigrants and citizens.

Religion Under Each State's Jurisdiction

U.S. Supreme Court Justice Joseph Story wrote in *Commentaries on the Constitution*, 1833: "The whole power over the subject of religion is left exclusively to the state governments, to be acted upon according to their own sense of justice and the state constitutions."

James Madison introduced the First Amendment in the first session of Congress. As the fourth President, Madison appointed Joseph Story to the Supreme Court in 1811. Story served on the Court 34 years and almost single-handedly founded Harvard Law School.

The "Constitution of the United States of America: Analysis and Interpretation," prepared by the Legislative Reference Service of the Library of Congress, stated about Justice Story:

> In his *Commentaries on the Constitution*, 1833, Justice Joseph Story asserted that the purpose of

the First Amendment was not to discredit the then existing state establishments of religion, but rather "to exclude from the national government all power to act on the subject." Justice Story continued: "In some of the states, Episcopalians constituted the predominant sect; in others, Presbyterians; in others, Congregationalists; in others, Quakers; and in others again, there was a close numerical rivalry among contending sects. It was impossible that there should not arise perpetual strife and perpetual jealousy on the subject of ecclesiastical ascendancy, if the national government were left free to create a religious establishment. The only security was in the abolishing the power. But this alone would have been an imperfect security, if it had not been followed up by a declaration of the right of the free exercise of religion . . . Thus, the whole power over the subject of religion is left exclusively to the state governments, to be acted upon according to their own sense of justice and the state constitutions."[7]

Like a race track with 13 lanes, some states expanded religious freedom quickly and others slowly. When the Constitution and Bill of Rights were ratified, some states allowed more religious freedom (i.e., Pennsylvania, Maryland, and Rhode Island) and others did not (i.e., Massachusetts, New Hampshire, and Connecticut).

Patricia U. Bonomi, Professor Emerita of New York University, wrote in "The Middle Colonies as the Birthplace of American Religious Pluralism":

Early American churchmen and churchwomen soon discovered that if they wanted to practice their beliefs unmolested in a diverse society, they had to grant the same right to others. This wisdom did not come easily.

In summary, when colonial settlers came over from England, it was as if America was a lifeboat amidst the sea of persecution. Over time, settlers put into effect the principle from the Sermon on the Mount, *"whatever you wish that others would do to you, do also to them."*

The lifeboat rescued:

- first Pilgrims and Puritans

- then Congregationalists, Presbyterians, Quakers, Dutch Reformed, Baptists, Lutherans, Reformed, Mennonite, French Huguenot, Methodist, Evangelical, Calvinist Reformed, Moravian, Seventh Day Baptist, Amish, Dunker, and Brethren

- then all Protestants

- then Catholics

- then Spanish-Portuguese Sephardic Jews

- then new Christian denominations and pseudo-Christian sects (Unitarian, Universalists, etc.)

- then German Ashkenazic Jews

- then monotheists

- then groups bordering on cults

- then polytheists (Chinese Buddhists, Indian Hindus)

- then finally atheists and Muslims.

Ironically, it seems the last ones in the boat consider it too crowded and are endeavoring to throw the first ones out—being intolerant of the same beliefs as those that founded the country.

States Expand Religious Liberty

At the time the Declaration of Independence and Constitution were written, Americans were:

- approximately 98 percent Protestant;

- a little less than 2 percent Catholic;

- just a tenth of one percent Jewish.

Patricia U. Bonomi stated that: "The colonists were about 98 percent Protestant."

Catholics were initially allowed in Maryland, Pennsylvania, and to a lesser extent in New York. Bishop John Carroll wrote to Rome in 1790:

> The thirteen provinces of North America rejected the yoke of England, they proclaimed, at the same time, freedom of conscience . . . Before this great event, the Catholic faith had penetrated two provinces only, Maryland and Pennsylvania. In all the others the laws against Catholics were in force.

Nine of the original thirteen state constitutions required office-holders be Protestant. For example, South Carolina, the eighth state to ratify the U.S. Constitution, stated in its 1778 State Constitution: "No person shall be eligible to a seat . . . unless he be of the **protestant** religion . . . The **Christian protestant** religion shall be deemed . . . the established religion of this state."

Some states were more liberal. Instead of requiring office holders to be Protestants, all that was necessary was to be a generic Christian or believe in the Bible.

Delaware, the first state to ratify the U.S. Constitution, stated in its 1776 State Constitution:

> Every person . . . appointed to any office . . . shall . . . subscribe . . . "I . . . profess faith in **God the Father**, and in **Jesus Christ** His only Son, and in the **Holy Ghost**, one God, blessed for evermore; and I do acknowledge the Holy Scriptures of the Old and New Testament to be given by Divine inspiration."

The various states, at their own speeds, chose to incrementally abolish such requirements.

Widespread Catholic Migration

When the Irish Potato Famine occurred in the early 1800s, millions of Irish Catholic immigrants flooded into the United States. The Catholic percentage of the population exploded from 2 percent to 20 percent.

There was an intense backlash with many states passing laws prohibiting tax dollars from going to Catholic schools. These were called "Blaine Amendments," named for Senator James G. Blaine from Maine.

Eventually, states accommodated Catholics by changing the requirement to hold office from "Protestant" to "Christian." North Carolina, for example, went from requiring office holders to be Protestant in 1776 to simply Christian in 1835. This was in effect until

1868 when all that was necessary was to believe in God.

Thus, North Carolina, the 12th state to ratify the U.S. Constitution, stated in its 1776 State Constitution:

> No person, who shall deny the being of **God** or the truth of the **protestant** religion, or the Divine authority either of the Old or New Testaments, or who shall hold religious principles incompatible with the freedom and safety of the state, shall be capable of holding . . . office.

The 1835 North Carolina Constitution stated:

> No person, who shall deny the being of God or the truth of the **Christian** religion, or the Divine authority either of the Old or New Testaments . . . shall be capable of holding . . . office.

Its 1868 Constitution said: "The following persons shall be disqualified for office: First, any person who shall deny the being of Almighty God." The 1971 (current) Constitution of North Carolina states: "Beneficent provision for the poor, the unfortunate, and the orphan is one of the first duties of a civilized and a Christian state."

Spanish and Portuguese Sephardic Jews had been in America since 1654, but in the early 1800s, a persecution of Ashkenazic Jews in Bavaria and Eastern Europe resulted in a quarter of a million Jews immigrating. America's Jewish population grew from a tenth of a percent to two percent.

Various states made accommodations, such as Maryland, which went from requiring office holders:

• be Christian in 1776

- to Christian and Jew in 1851

- to Christian and believing in God in 1864

- and finally, to simply believing in God in 1867.

State Churches Among the States

Justice Hugo Lafayette Black wrote in *Engel v. Vitale* (June 25, 1962): "As late as the time of the Revolutionary War, there were established Churches in at least eight of the thirteen former colonies and established religions in at least four of the other five."

John K. Wilson wrote in "Religion Under the State Constitutions 1776–1800," "An establishment of religion, in terms of direct tax aid to Churches, was the situation in nine of the thirteen colonies on the eve of the American revolution."[8]

Congressman James Meacham of Vermont, reporting for the House Judiciary Committee in 1854, stated:

> At the adoption of the Constitution, we believe every state—certainly 10 of the 13—provided as regularly for the support of the church as for the support of the government: one, Virginia, had the system of tithes. Down to the Revolution, every colony did sustain religion in some form. It was deemed peculiarly proper that the religion of liberty should be upheld by a free people. Had the people, during the Revolution, had a suspicion of any attempt to war against Christianity, that Revolution would have been strangled in its cradle.[9]

Gustave de Beaumont, who traveled with Alexis de Tocqueville, wrote in *Marie ou L'Esclavage aux E'tas-Unis* (1835):

All of the American constitutions exhort the citizens to practice religious worship as a safeguard both to good morals and to public liberties. In the United States, the law is never atheistic ... All of the American constitutions proclaim freedom of conscience and the liberty and equality of all the confessions. . . . There is not a single state where public opinion and the customs of the inhabitants do not forcefully constrain an obligation to these beliefs.[10]

French political writer Alexis de Tocqueville wrote in *Democracy in America* (1840):

The sects that exist in the United States are innumerable . . . Moreover, all the sects of the United States are comprised within the great unity of Christianity, and Christian morality is everywhere the same . . . In the United States Christian sects are infinitely diversified and perpetually modified; but Christianity itself is a fact so irresistibly established, that no one undertakes either to attack or to defend it.

"The Constitution of the United States of America: Analysis and Interpretation" stated:

Justice Story contended, the establishment clause, while it inhibited Congress from giving preference to any denomination of the Christian faith, was not intended to withdraw the Christian religion as a whole from the protection of Congress. Justice Joseph Story continued: "Probably at the time of the adoption of the Constitution, and of the Amendment to it now under consideration, the general if not the universal sentiment in America was, that Christianity ought to receive encouragement from the state so far as was not incompatible with the private rights of conscience and the freedom of religious worship. Any attempt to level all religions, and make it a matter of state policy to hold all in utter indifference, would have created universal disapprobation, if not universal indignation."[11]

What all this means is that over time, America became dedicated to a non-sectarian model. But that is a far cry from secularism. Today, many people confuse those two concepts.

John Bouvier's *Law Dictionary* stated in its definition of "religion":

The Constitution of the United States provides that "Congress shall make no law respecting an establishment of religion or prohibiting the free exercise thereof." This provision and that relating to religious tests are limitations upon the power of the Congress only . . . The Christian religion is, of course, recognized by the government, yet . . . the preservation of religious liberty is left to the states.[12]

U.S. Supreme Court Justice John Paul Stevens wrote in *Wallace v. Jaffree* (June 4, 1985):

The individual's freedom to choose his own creed is the counterpart of his right to refrain from accepting the creed established by the majority. At one time it was thought that this right merely proscribed the preference of one Christian sect over another, but would not require equal respect for the conscience of the infidel, the atheist, or the adherent of a non-

Christian faith.

President Calvin Coolidge stated on May 3, 1925:

> Many and scattered colonial communities . . . had been planted along the Atlantic seaboard . . . There were well-nigh as many divergencies of religious faith as there were of origin, politics and geography . . . From its beginning, the new continent had seemed destined to be the home of religious tolerance. Those who claimed the right of individual choice for themselves finally had to grant it to others.

First Amendment

Ten days after his Inauguration, President Washington wrote to the United Baptist Churches of Virginia, May 10, 1789:

> If I could have entertained the slightest apprehension that the Constitution framed by the Convention, where I had the honor to preside, might possibly endanger the religious rights of any ecclesiastical Society, certainly I would never have placed my signature to it.

During the debates of the Bill of Rights, Rep. Thomas Tucker of South Carolina made a motion to completely strike the establishment clause from the First Amendment, as he thought it could be misapplied to preempt the religious clauses existing in the various state constitutions.

Rep. Roger Sherman of Connecticut thought the First Amendment was completely unnecessary, as the state delegates, when writing the U.S. Constitution, only gave the Federal Government specific powers, and authority over religion was not one of them.

While Thomas Jefferson was not there when the First Amendment was written and adapted, his views are worth noting. Jefferson viewed the "wall" as limiting the Federal Government from "inter-meddling" in church affairs, as he wrote to Samuel Miller, January 23, 1808:

> I consider the government of the United States as interdicted [prohibited] by the Constitution from inter-meddling with religious institutions, their doctrines, discipline, or exercises. . . . Every religious society has a right to determine for itself the times for these exercises, and the objects proper for them, according to their own particular tenets.

Wall of Separation Between Church and State

Earlier we saw how the Puritan Rev. Roger Williams spoke of the metaphor of a "wall of separation," separating church and state. Jumping ahead to Jefferson's time, our third president also spoke of a wall of separation between church and state. This is found in a letter he wrote to the Danbury Baptists.

The context of his letter is that since Connecticut had established the Congregational denomination, the Danbury Baptist Association felt disadvantaged. They wrote to Jefferson, October 7, 1801:

> Sir . . . Our sentiments are uniformly on the side of religious liberty:
>
> - that religion is at all times and places a matter between God and individuals,
>
> - that no man ought to suffer in name, person or effects on account of his religious Opinions,
>
> - that the legitimate power of civil government extends no further than to punish the man who

works ill to his neighbor.

Jefferson replied with his famous letter, January 1, 1802, agreeing with the Danbury Baptists, repeating sections of their letter almost verbatim:

> Gentlemen . . . Believing **with you**
>
> - that religion is a matter which lies solely between man and his God,
>
> - that he owes account to none other for faith or his worship,
>
> - that the legislative powers of government reach actions only, and not opinions,
>
> I contemplate with solemn reverence that act of the whole American people which declared that their legislature should "make no law respecting an establishment of religion, or prohibiting the free exercise thereof," thus building a wall of separation between church and state.

Jefferson continued:

> Adhering to this expression of the supreme will of the nation in behalf of the rights of conscience, I shall see with sincere satisfaction the progress of those sentiments which tend to restore man to all his natural rights, convinced he has no natural right in opposition to his social duties. I reciprocate your kind prayers for the protection and blessing of the

common Father and Creator of man, and tender
you for yourselves and your religious association,
assurances of my high respect and esteem.

At the end of the letter, Jefferson asks them to pray to God for
him, and likewise he commits to pray for them. Jefferson does not
advocate a separation of God and state, but rather a separation of the
institution of the church from the institution of the state.

President Calvin Coolidge stated at the 150th anniversary of the
Declaration of Independence, July 4, 1926: "This preaching reached
the neighborhood of Thomas Jefferson, who acknowledged that his
'best ideas of democracy' had been secured at church meetings."

Like dealing a deck of cards in a card game, the states dealt
to the Federal Government jurisdiction over a few specific things,
such as providing for the common defense and regulating interstate
commerce, but the rest of the cards were held by the states.

Jefferson explained in his Second Inaugural Address, March 4,
1805:

> In matters of religion I have considered that its free
> exercise is placed by the Constitution independent
> of the powers of the General [Federal] Government.
> I have therefore undertaken, on no occasion, to
> prescribe the religious exercise suited to it; but have
> left them, as the Constitution found them, under
> the direction and discipline of state and church
> authorities by the several religious societies.

That is why as Governor of Virginia, he had no problem declaring a Day of Prayer, but he would not do the same thing as President
of the United States.

James Madison made a journal entry, June 12, 1788:

> There is not a shadow of right in the General [Federal] Government to inter-meddle with religion . . . The subject is, for the honor of America, perfectly free and unshackled. The government has no jurisdiction over it.

States jealously guarded their freedom of religion, leading them to send representatives to the First Session of Congress where they passed the First Amendment: "Congress shall make no law respecting an establishment of religion, or prohibiting the free exercise thereof . . ."

If they could have seen into the future that judges would usurp power by making laws from the bench, or that Presidents would usurp power by making laws through executive orders and regulations, the founders most likely would have worded the First Amendment: "Congress, the Supreme Court, and the President shall make no law respecting an establishment of religion, or prohibiting the free exercise thereof."

The First Amendment put two specific handcuffs on the wrists of the Federal Government:

1. The Federal Government could not establish one official national denomination, as this would conflict with the many states established denominations. This is called "the establishment clause."

2. The Federal Government could not prohibit individuals within the states from enjoying the free exercise of their religion. This is called "the free exercise clause."

What Changed?

James H. Landman, director of community programs for the American Bar Association Division for Public Education in Chicago says:

For most of our history, the majority of Americans have practiced some form of Christian Protestantism . . . In 1925 . . . public schools . . . still played a significant role in inculcating Anglo-Protestant moral values."[13]

Three events changed this:

- FIRST, the Irish Potato Famine in the early 1800s resulted in millions of Irish Catholics immigrating to America. A backlash against Catholics resulted in laws being passed called "anti-sectarian" ordinances such as the "Blaine Amendments," which prevented state tax money from going to Catholic schools. The tax-supported public schools of the time were thoroughly Protestant Christian.

- SECOND, in 1868, the 14th Amendment was passed to force southern Democrat states to grant rights to freed slaves. When concerns arose during the debates whether the 14th Amendment might be reinterpreted by the Federal Government to usurp jurisdiction away from states in other areas, Rep. John Bingham of Ohio, who introduced the Amendment, replied: "I repel the suggestion . . . that the Amendment will take away from any state any right that belongs to it." Yet, the usurping process began nonetheless.

- THIRD, in 1859, Charles Darwin published his book, *On the Origin of Species*. His theory that species could evolve inspired a political theorist named Herbert Spencer, who coined the term "survival of the fittest." Spencer advocated applying Darwin's evolutionary theory to other areas of the academic enterprise.

Beginning in 1870, Harvard Law Professor Christopher Columbus Langdell pioneered applying evolution to the legal process. He innovated the "case precedent" method of practicing law, which made it no longer necessary to study the intent of those who wrote the Constitution. Instead, jurists would just look at the most recent cases and expand its reach a little at a time. No other law school in the nation at that time taught this.

Evolutionary "Case Precedent" Method

Evolutionary law grew in acceptance, especially after 1902 when Harvard graduate Oliver Wendell Holmes, Jr., was put on the Supreme Court. His biographer described in *The Justice from Beacon Hill: The Life and Times of Oliver Wendell Holmes* Holmes's theory of "legal realism," which, he said:

> . . . shook the little world of lawyers and judges who had been raised on Blackstone's theory that the law, given by God Himself, was immutable and eternal and judges had only to discover its contents. It took some years for them to come around to the view that the law was flexible, responsive to changing social and economic climates . . . Holmes had . . . broken new intellectual trails . . . demonstrating that the corpus of the law was neither *ukase* [an edict] from God nor derived from Nature, but . . . was a constantly evolving thing, a response to the continually developing social and economic environment.

Supreme Court Justices began to fall into two general categories: 1) those who hold that laws should keep the meaning of those who wrote them, and 2) those who hold that laws can evolve to have new meanings at the justice's discretion.

The evolutionary "case-precedent" method provided a way for activist justices to use the 14th Amendment, together with an "expanded" interpretation of the "commerce clause," to side-step the Constitutional means of changing the Constitution through the Amendment process. Soon federal judges began to take jurisdiction away from the states over issues such as unions, strikes, railroads, farming, polygamy, freedom of speech, freedom of the press, and freedom of assembly.

Religion remained under each state's jurisdiction until Franklin D. Roosevelt put the former KKK member Senator Hugo Black on the Supreme Court.

Like President Roosevelt, Justice Black concentrated power in the Federal Government, most notably in the case of *Everson v. Board of Education* (1947). Catholic students in New Jersey were getting bus rides to Catholic schools. A lawsuit based on "anti-sectarian," anti-Catholic Blaine Amendments attempted to stop the bus rides. It was lost on the state level, but was appealed to the Supreme Court.

Justice Black creatively applied the evolutionary "case precedent" method with an expanded view of the 14th Amendment, to remove religion from states' jurisdiction and put it under Federal purview.

Thomas Jefferson predicted judicial overreach in a letter to Charles Hammond in 1821:

> The germ of dissolution of our Federal Government is in . . . the Federal Judiciary . . . working like gravity by night and by day, gaining a little today and a little tomorrow, and advancing its noiseless step like a thief, over the field of jurisdiction, until all shall be usurped from the states."

Courts Recognize Other "Religions"

Federal courts accelerated this process. In 1957, the Washington

Ethical Society wanted tax-exempt status the same as a church. The IRS denied them, but the Supreme Court declared "ethical culture" a religion and allowed them tax-exemption.

In 1961, Roy Torcaso wanted to be a notary public in Maryland but did not want to say "so help me God" at the end of his oath as he was an atheist. When the state denied him the job, the Supreme Court overruled, deciding that secular humanism was also a religion.

During the Vietnam War, Elliot Welsh wanted to be a draft dodger claiming religious conscientious objector status as an atheist. When the Army did not accept this, the Supreme Court stepped in, stating: "We think it clear that the beliefs which prompted his objection occupy the same place in his life as the belief in a traditional deity holds in the lives of his friends, the Quakers."

In 2005, James Kaufman wanted to use a room while in the Jackson Correctional Prison for a non-Bible study. When the state denied him, the 7th Circuit Court of Appeals overruled, stating: "A religion need not be based on a belief in the existence of a supreme being . . . Atheism is Kaufman's religion."

Once federal courts recognized atheism as a "religion," in order to not prefer one "religion" over another, they kicked God out. Ironically, this resulted in the Federal Government establishing, by its own definition, the "religion of atheism."

Supreme Court Justice Potter Stewart warned in his dissent of *Abington Township v. Schempp* (1963):

> The state may not establish a 'religion of secularism' in the sense of affirmatively opposing or showing hostility to religion, thus 'preferring those who believe in no religion over those who do believe' . . . Refusal to permit religious exercises thus is seen, not as the realization of state neutrality, but rather as the establishment of a religion of secularism.

Freedom *Of* Religions Versus Freedom *From* Religion

U.S. District Court stated in *Crockett v. Sorenson*, (W.D. Va., 1983):

> The First Amendment was never intended to insulate our public institutions from any mention of God, the Bible or religion. When such insulation occurs, another religion, such as secular humanism, is effectively established.

Ronald Reagan described this on the National Day of Prayer, May 6, 1982: "Well-meaning Americans in the name of freedom have taken freedom away. For the sake of religious tolerance, they've forbidden religious practice."

Reagan added in a question and answer session, October 13, 1983: "The First Amendment has been twisted to the point that freedom of religion is in danger of becoming freedom from religion."

Reagan addressed the Alabama State Legislature, March 15, 1982: "The First Amendment of the Constitution was not written to protect the people of this country from religious values; it was written to protect religious values from government tyranny."

CHAPTER 5

The State of Religious Liberty in Modern America

by David Gibbs, III

. . . where the Spirit of the Lord is, there is freedom.
2 CORINTHIANS 3:17

W hen the President of the United States delivers his annual State of the Union address to Congress every year, he generally begins that speech by saying "The state of our union is _____." So we begin this article by saying, "The state of religious liberty in America is, at this moment, in peril."

We observe this peril in several contrasting events. When a famous dress designer said, following President Donald Trump's election, that he would refuse to use his creative talents to design a dress for the First Lady because he did not agree with President Trump's views, he was applauded and seen as a courageous figure by many. At the same time, when a Colorado cake baker and a Washington State florist refused to use their creative talents to participate in a same-sex wedding because their religious beliefs recognize marriage as only between a man and woman, they were called "bigots," received massive fines, and were hauled into court on charges of discrimination.

Similarly, when a young football player, Colin Kaepernick, "took a knee" on the sidelines during the National Anthem to protest alleged racism by police, he was hailed as a First Amendment free speech hero. Many others later followed his example without penalty. Earlier, however, when another young football player, Tim Tebow, "took a knee" on the sidelines to pray before a game, he was criticized and told such displays were not permitted on the football field.

America's First Freedom

Religious liberty is the subject of the first phrase in America's First Amendment list of freedoms for an important reason. America's founders believed that religious liberty was America's First Freedom—the one on which all other freedoms were secured. The first phrase of the First Amendment states: "Congress shall make no law respecting an establishment of religion, or prohibiting the free exercise thereof; . . ."

Most Americans no longer understand the true meaning and importance of religious liberty, which is declining in modern America. For instance, during President Barack Obama's eight years in office, he often mischaracterized the First Amendment by referring, not to the freedoms of religion or religious expression, which actually are protected in the First Amendment, but instead, to a nebulous "freedom of worship." Others followed his lead when speaking about what America's founders considered to be our nation's very first foundational liberty. While it may initially seem like a minor semantic alteration, confusing "freedom of worship" with "freedom of religion" makes a very big difference.

Freedom to worship indicates an activity that takes place generally in a church or synagogue, perhaps even in a mosque or temple these days in America. Religious worship is generally a private activity practiced behind closed doors where non-worshippers do not observe it. Article 52 of the former Soviet Union's constitution, for instance, protected "religious worship," but true religious liberty—the right to live out one's religious beliefs in everyday life—was denied to citizens of that atheist state. Those who took their religion outside the walls of the church were persecuted.

America's first freedom—religious liberty—is not intended to take place only in a church or other place of worship. Religion is intended to be an organizing principle of life itself. As such, it is intended to march right out into the public square and influence every area of society, government, and culture.

While the etymology of the word "religion" is somewhat obscure, many tie it back to the Latin word, *ligare*, which means "to bind." "Re-ligion" then, or "re-*ligare*," thus means to tie something back together or to reorganize something based on a consistent order. This understanding of religion is more akin to *The Theory of Everything*, the title of Stephen Hawkings' 2014 cinematic biography. Religion, then, is the opposite of analysis. The process of analysis involves taking something apart to see how it works, while religion involves tying things back together to work in an ordered manner.

The Bible tells us in Colossians 1:17 that Christ is the "one who holds all things together." There is even an interesting recent medical discovery that seems to biologically mirror that spiritual reality. Scientists have discovered something called "laminin" in the human body, an adhesion protein molecule that literally **holds** the body **together.** Scientists have described this molecule as having a cross-like or *cruciform* shape. In the same way that biologically "laminin" holds the human body together, Biblical Christianity provides the order needed to hold together or to bind (*ligare*) all of life and society together.

Judeo-Christian Origins of American Law and Government

Of course, America's founders knew nothing about biological "laminin." But they did know that their new nation needed to be organized and ordered around principles found in the Judeo-Christian religion. They began with their affirmation in the Declaration of Independence that the Biblical God is the Creator, that all mankind is created equal, and that God, not government, is the Giver of rights, which every government is then required to secure for every individual.

When Judge Roy Moore was elected as Alabama's GOP Senatorial candidate, Chuck Todd, host of NBC's *Meet the Press*, demonstrated America's general ignorance about the origin of constitutional rights. Todd criticized Judge Moore's public statement that "[o]ur rights don't come from government, they don't come from the Bill of Rights, they come from Almighty God." Todd said, "He [Judge Moore] doesn't appear to believe in the Constitution as it's written." That statement summed up the unfortunate fact that Americans in general have forgotten what their ancestors only a generation or two ago understood very well. The Declaration of Independence, which is America's foundational document on which the Constitution is based, quite clearly proclaims the truth of Judge Moore's statement. The constitutional ignorance of news anchor Chuck Todd and many other Americans in the 21st century is, indeed, alarming.

The Declaration of Independence clearly states: "We hold these truths to be self-evident, that all men are created equal, that they are endowed **by their Creator** with certain unalienable Rights, that among these are Life, Liberty and the pursuit of Happiness." [Emphasis added.] It is significant that President Obama often quoted this sentence from the Declaration while eliminating the words italicized above. This elimination also represents the prevailing viewpoint of those judges and jurists who believe in a "living constitution"—one that American courts can twist into any shape that represents the judge's own personal, progressive views. Chuck Todd may have been listening to President Obama and other liberal progressives, rather than taking the time to read America's founding documents for himself—something far too many modern Americans have apparently overlooked as well.

That same Declaration also states that the Rights of all people are, and forever will be, innate and unalienable because they were established based upon "the Law of Nature and of Nature's God." At the time the Declaration of Independence was written, that phrase clearly referred to God's natural law (the "Law of Nature") and to God's self-revelation in the Holy Scriptures of the Judeo-Christian religion (the "Law of Nature's God").

That important concept is the reason why "religious liberty" was considered by America's founders to be the First Freedom. Our founding documents—the Declaration of Independence, the Constitution, the Bill of Rights—were organized and ordered around religious principles found in the Judeo-Christian scriptures. The Judeo-Christian religion is a religion that permits individuals the freedom to choose for themselves whether or how to serve the Creator God of the Universe. That freedom must then follow through in the rest of an organized and ordered society and government by granting the additional First Amendment freedoms of speech, press, association and petition, which allow individuals to freely practice that first foundational religious liberty and perform their duties to their Creator God as they see fit. Nations that do not recognize a Creator God and religious liberty will generally deny other liberties to their citizens as well. Americans must understand the reality that if religious liberty goes, it will take all other constitutional freedoms with it.

1983—The Year of the Bible

Twentieth century Americans, for the most part, continued to understand the important foundational Judeo-Christian principles of their nation. In 1983, President Ronald Reagan led the nation in celebrating "The International Year of the Bible."

A few years later, on May 25, 1987, *Time* magazine published an article called "*Looking to Its Roots*," which stated:

> Ours [America] is the only country deliberately founded on a good idea. That good idea combines a commitment to man's inalienable rights with the Calvinist belief in an ultimate moral right and sinful man's obligation to do good. These articles of faith, embodied in the Declaration of Independence and in the Constitution, literally govern our lives today.

Even the secular news media in the 1980s acknowledged the Judeo-Christian origins of America, the only nation in the world that was founded on a religious ideal rather than on physical, ethnic, or cultural ties. Columnist Mona Charen later observed in a September 2003 issue of *Insight* magazine that "Judeo-Christian values are not being 'imposed' upon the American public; they are at the root of the civilized society our forefathers founded." America has seen a tremendous shift away from that truth in law, politics, and culture over the last few decades.

America's Biblical Founders

John Adams, American founder, lawyer, and our nation's second president, clearly understood that America was established as a uniquely Judeo-Christian nation, and that this nation would not long survive if its religious foundation was ever removed. Although Adams himself did not attend the Constitutional Convention in Philadelphia in 1787, the vast majority of colonial delegates who did attend shared his foundational Judeo-Christian beliefs. In a letter dated 11 October 1798, Adams said this of the Constitution drafted at that meeting:

> [W]e have no government armed with power capable
> of contending with human passions unbridled by
> morality and religion. Avarice, ambition, revenge,
> or gallantry, would break the strongest cords of our
> Constitution as a whale goes through a net. Our
> Constitution was made only for a moral and religious
> people. It is wholly inadequate to the government of
> any other.

President John Adams was also clearly convinced that the strong
influence of Christianity had shaped American republicanism. He
wrote to President Thomas Jefferson on June 28, 1813:

> The general Principles, on which the Fathers Achieved
> Independence, were the only Principles in which that
> beautiful Assembly of young Gentlemen could Unite,
> and these Principles only could be intended by them
> in their Address, or by me in my Answer. And what
> were these general Principles? I answer, the general
> Principles of Christianity, in which all those Sects
> were united: And the general Principles of English
> and American Liberty, in which all those young Men
> United, and which had United all Parties in America
> in Majorities sufficient to assert and maintain her
> Independence.[1]

America's government was intended by our founders to rest
on the stable support of a three-legged stool. One of America's first
laws as a new nation, passed in Congress at the same time the Bill of
Rights was enacted, identified these three legs as religion, morality,
and knowledge (education). This law, the Northwest Ordinance
of 1789, was adopted to assist in the formation of new states and
territories in the West. It declared that "RELIGION, MORALITY,

AND KNOWLEDGE" were "necessary to good government and the happiness of mankind."

Our first president, George Washington, in his 1796 Farewell Address, warned citizens of the importance of preserving America's religious foundation when he admonished them to "with caution indulge the supposition that morality can be maintained without religion." While these founders did not dictate any particular sect that must be followed, they did encourage Americans to practice their Judeo-Christian faith—even by governmental actions such as printing Bibles for Christian missions to the West.

The majority of America's founders were professing Christians, a fact many modern Americans would like to erase. Only Benjamin Franklin and James Wilson of Pennsylvania were known to be deists, while Hugh Williamson of North Carolina and James McClurg of Virginia may also have been non-Trinitarian. At most, 5.5 percent of those attending the 1787 Constitutional Convention were not professing Christians.

Political science professors Charles S. Hyneman and Donald S. Lutz conducted an examination of some 15,000 documents, including several thousand political books, pamphlets, etc. written during America's founding era between 1760 and 1805. This 1983 study found 3,154 citations or references to other sources, most of which were references to the Bible. On average, during that particular half century, they determined that 34 percent of political literary citations came from the Bible. In fact, far more often than they quote any particular individual, the political writers of that era quoted the Bible as the basis for their political views.

Sir William Blackstone's *Commentaries on the Laws of England*, written in the late 1760s, initially provided the basis for America's laws. The *Commentaries* were studied by lawyers and judges and were used by them as legal resources well into the 19th Century. This early legal work was filled with Biblical principles and references that undergirded American law for more than a century after 1787.

It is unmistakable that the vast majority of America's founders were professing Christians whose views on politics, government, and law were influenced directly and positively by the Bible. The constitutions and laws of those states that united to form the United States of America were all based on the Creator God and the Bible.

America's founders based their Declaration of Independence, as well as their Constitution and America's laws, on religious principles found in the Scriptures of the Old and New Testaments. In fact, when the early colonists were protesting colonial tyranny by the King of England, a prominent revolutionary cry was "No King but King Jesus." America's revolutionaries wanted to organize their new government according to the religion of the Bible. They wanted to tie everything together in an order that was based upon the Creator God and the Judeo-Christian religion. The Judeo-Christian religious Scriptures, they knew, were based on the concept that every individual has the freedom, not only to "worship" God, but to perform their religious duties to their Creator God in the public square as well.

America Is a Christian Nation

In the 1892 case of *Church of the Holy Trinity v. United States*, Justice David Brewer, who wrote the opinion for the Court, summarized the state of the law at that time and demonstrated decisively that America is a Christian nation. After discussing the specific facts of the case, Justice Brewer continued for page after page to explore the question of whether America was a Christian nation. Justice Brewer's answer to his own question was a resoundingly clear "Yes." He wrote: "This is a religious people. This is historically true."

Justice Brewer came to that conclusion after reviewing various important historical documents and events in American history up to that time, including the Christian influence on explorer Christopher Columbus; the Christian influence on the early colonial British grants, charters, and colonial constitutions that all acknowledged God and His purpose and influence in founding this new nation to freely worship God and proselytize the natives; on the constitutions of the original states that all acknowledged God as they joined the union; on the Declaration of Independence with its freedoms granted by the Creator God of the Bible; on the Constitution, which presumes the existence of God and the truth of the Bible; and on several previous affirmative decisions of lower courts.

Justice Brewer then declared that, while all types of religious expression are protected in America, the religion of the American people is not "the religion of Mahomet [Mohammed] or of the Grand Lama; and for this plain reason, [the law] assumes that we are a Christian people, and the morality of the country is deeply engrafted upon Christianity." Justice Brewer concluded his far-reaching decision by stating:

> If we pass beyond these matters to a view of American life as expressed by its laws, its business, its customs and its society, we find everywhere a clear recognition of the same truth . . . that this is a Christian nation.

If We Can Keep It

It must be clearly acknowledged that America's founders intended to establish this nation on the foundation of the Judeo-Christian religion. If modern America loses that faith and restricts the religious liberty of those who still practice that faith, which contains the true founding spirit of America, can this nation long survive? That is the question we 21st century Americans must ask ourselves. And that is the famous question Benjamin Franklin addressed as he left Philadelphia's Independence Hall in the summer of 1787 after the Constitution had been drafted.

The story is told that when Benjamin Franklin emerged from the building that day, he was met by a Mrs. Powell of Philadelphia. Mrs. Powell is said to have pointedly put an important question to Dr. Franklin. "Well doctor," she asked, "what have we got? A republic or a monarchy?" Franklin immediately responded, "A republic, madam—*if you can keep it.*"

It is beginning to appear that after nearly 250 years, Dr. Franklin's warning may now be falling on deaf ears. America may be losing, not only its foundational Judeo-Christian heritage, but its taste for religious liberty entirely—and with it, perhaps also its taste for liberty in general. Colleges are shutting down free speech with which they disagree. Our laws no longer protect everyone equally. Those in power are not held to the same standard as others. Our free press has become "fake news" which cannot be trusted by its readers and viewers. Christians are being prosecuted for discrimination just for continuing to follow their Christian faith as it has been practiced for more than 2,000 years.

It is important to remember that the Biblical concept of liberty is not the equivalent of a "license" to live as licentiously as we please. While promoting the concept of granting to each individual the freedom to decide whether or how to serve their Creator God, the Bible also condemns the sort of license—the Bible calls it "licentiousness"—that seems to have become the new god of modern America.

President John Adams, quoted previously in this article, also noted in a June 21, 1776, letter to his cousin, Zabdiel, a pastor:

> Statesmen may plan and speculate for Liberty, but it is Religion and Morality alone, which can establish the Principles upon which Freedom can securely stand. . . . The only foundation of a free Constitution, is pure Virtue, and if this cannot be inspired into our People, in a great Measure, than they have it now, They may change their Rulers, and the forms of Government, but they will not obtain a lasting Liberty.

This warning should carry great weight today in America as our religious liberty is in peril and our foundational Judeo-Christian national ethic is in jeopardy of disappearing entirely.

Separating Church and State

It was not until the mid-20th century (1947 to be exact) that the U.S. Supreme Court came up with the notion that America should practice a radical version of separation of church and state. Prior to this time, it was understood that America already did practice a form of separation of church and state. However, within that separation, it was understood that both the church and the state were intended to separately operate under God, as our Pledge of Allegiance still testifies: "One nation, under God, indivisible, with liberty and justice for all."

In 1947, the United States Supreme Court in *Everson v. Board of Education* erected a high "wall of separation" between church and state, language that has since been increasingly interpreted by our courts as a prohibition on allowing religion to influence the actions of government in any manner. This concept is entirely antithetical to America's foundational freedoms, which were based on the Judeo-Christian religion. America's founders, as we have seen, intended that God and the Bible's notion of liberty would be the backbone for the nation.

Until the 20th century, every president, every citizen, and every school child celebrated those Biblical principles on which America had been founded. However, beginning with this 1947 radical "separation of church and state" concept, our courts have used this court-invented doctrine to remove more and more of America's original dependence upon God and to attempt to make the United States an atheistic nation that does not recognize God or religion at all.

What the removal of God and the Biblical underpinnings of America's culture, government, and law has done is to also remove America's original commitment to religious liberty—and, in fact, to undermine all individual liberty as well. The Bible and its notions of religious liberty were considered to be America's First Freedom. Of course, it must be noted that as our nation grew from childhood to adulthood, its basic understanding of the equality of all under God increased and expanded. In so doing, the nation moved even closer to the basic equality of the entire human race, as understood in the Judeo-Christian scriptures. However, as that freedom has begun to erode, we are beginning to see the erosion of all liberty in this nation once truly known as the "land of the free."

The Mystery Passage

It is undeniable that many in America, including those on the Highest Court in our land, seem to have forgotten the *religare* (religion) that previously bound Americans together. This abandonment of the truth of America's founding order in the Judeo-Christian religion was made all too clear when the United States Supreme Court reaffirmed its pro-abortion/pro-choice standard in 1992 in the case of *Planned Parenthood v. Casey.*

There is a particular passage from the *Casey* decision that has since become known in legal and philosophical circles as "the mystery passage." In articulating this passage, the Court completely changed the nation's original Divine orientation of liberty by stating that the constitutional right to "liberty" is so expansive that "[a]t the heart of liberty is the right to define one's own concept of existence, of meaning, of the universe, and of the mystery of human life." In this "mystery passage," the Court declared that every individual has the right to determine the boundaries of his own liberty and, thereby, to define his own religious and moral standards in whatever way he chooses—completely free of any continuing ties to America's founding principles in the Creator God of the Bible as the Giver of rights and the foundation for an ordered American life. Government then seemingly becomes obligated to legally recognize whatever bizarre notions of liberty any individual might concoct.

Judge Robert Bork was the jurist Congress famously rejected

for the U.S. Supreme Court in 1987—leading to use of the word "borked" to describe when nominees are rejected based merely on political grounds through defamation and vilification. Judge Bork later commented on *Casey*'s "mystery passage" in the context of a discussion on euthanasia in his 1996 book, *Slouching Toward Gomorrah: Modern Liberalism and American Decline*. Judge Bork, who was noted for his humor, remarked:

> One would think that grown men and women, purporting to practice an intellectual profession, would themselves choose to die with dignity, right in the courtroom, before writing sentences like those. They mean nothing and were intended to mean nothing. They were intended, through grandiose rhetoric, to appeal to a free-floating spirit of radical autonomy.[2]

In proclaiming this radical declaration of a pregnant woman's right to become a god unto herself, the Supreme Court in *Casey* began to pull at the very covenantal threads that hold any society together. If America can no longer maintain a generally accepted societal standard of morality and civil conduct, but begins to legally allow every person the "liberty" to determine that standard entirely individually, our society will topple under the heavy weight of diversity run amok.

John Locke was a Christian Enlightenment thinker who greatly influenced America's founders. He noted that the first act of any civil society is a covenant whereby each individual relinquishes his natural and private rights to judge and execute the law of nature (i.e., God's law, mentioned in the Declaration of Independence) and transfers such powers to civil government's judicial and executive powers. In the absence of such a covenant, however, it is impossible to maintain political and societal order. Some other kind of order might evolve from the ensuing general chaos, and other forms of contracts can be undertaken, but they will not result in binding the society together.

It can be argued that more recent decisions of the United States Supreme Court, like "the mystery passage" in *Casey*, have placed America in a position where her original covenant of union, based upon the Judeo-Christian religion, is dissolving and civil society as we have known it may find it difficult to continue. Judge Bork expressed his aversion to this potential unraveling of American order through our Courts' extreme judicial activism. He observed again in *Gomorrah* regarding "the mystery passage":

> Judicial radical individualism weakens or destroys the authority of what sociologists call "intermediate institutions"—families, schools, business organizations, private associations, mayors, city councils, governors, state legislatures—that stand between the individual and the national government and its bureaucracies. All of this has happened within the lifetimes of many Americans. We are worse off because of it, and none of it was commanded or contemplated by the Constitution.[3]

Judge Bork correctly described the current direction of American liberal progressive law. In this context, the answer to Dr. Franklin's admonition "if we can keep it" is that 21st century America is not doing a very good job of "keeping it."

An Untethered Notion of Liberty

Since the *Casey* "mystery passage" entered American law, we have seen the U.S. Supreme Court take this individualized notion of the right for each person "to define one's own concept of existence, of meaning, of the universe, and of the mystery of human life" to the extreme in the case of *Obergefell v. Hodges*. In that 2015 case, the

Court entirely redefined the concept of marriage, an institution that had stood for thousands of years as a foundational principle of an ordered society. While this is the latest culmination of the Court's declaration of the "mystery" of a completely untethered notion of liberty, there is no guarantee it will be the last.

With *Obergefell*, "the mystery passage" concept has now crossed the line to actually undermine the foundational order of the Judeo-Christian Biblical religion on which America was founded. The *Obergefell* decision has specifically provided the basis on which to undermine religious liberty entirely. The notion now is that if the Judeo-Christian faith (or any faith) objects to the redefinition of marriage, it is that faith, with its attendant religious liberty, that must be suppressed and driven out of American society and culture, not the redefinition of marriage.

To add insult to injury, it now appears that the only ordering principle of society that an American is <u>not</u> permitted to use "to define one's own concept of existence, of meaning, of the universe, and of the mystery of human life" (the words used by the Court in the *Casey* decision) is America's founding principles in the Judeo-Christian religion. When President Donald Trump nominated Judge Amy Barrett, a Catholic law professor, for the Seventh U.S. Circuit Court of Appeals, Senators Dianne Feinstein (D-CA) and Dick Durbin (D-IL) actually questioned whether an individual could be a practicing Christian and a judge at the same time. Judge Barrett had previously stated in a 1997-98 *Marquette Law Review* article on capital punishment that "judges cannot—nor should they try to—align our legal system with the Church's moral teaching whenever the two diverge," a statement that is itself entirely antithetical to our nation's founding Judeo-Christian religious principles. Nevertheless, even that statement was still too much for these progressive Senators who considered that Judge Barrett's religious faith entirely disqualified her for the job. Sen. Feinstein later defended her questioning of Judge Barrett by insisting that religious believers like Barrett are not able to be objective on the bench.

Similarly, when President Trump nominated Russell Vought, a practicing Christian, as deputy director of the Office of Management and Budget, Senator Bernie Sanders (D-VT) thought it was appropriate to quiz Vought about a theological blog post he had written defending the Christian view of salvation. The obvious end of these modern Senatorial inquisitions is that while you may be a Christian privately, do <u>not</u> bring your faith into the public square or into a government workplace. These Senators are now attempting to impose an (anti) religious test on all government nominees by insisting that no sincere and practicing Christian is qualified to serve in government. Apparently, only those whose definition of the "concept of existence, of meaning, of the universe, and of the mystery of human life" is non-Christian, or perhaps even anti-Christian, are now qualified to serve in government.

Overthrowing All Liberty

Today, we have demonstrations on our college campuses advocating "free speech for me, but not for thee." If speech contradicts certain politically correct progressive viewpoints, the notion is now promoted that such speech may not be heard. Activist LGBT groups promote the principle in liberal, progressive courts that if religious theology does not conform to LGBT notions of sexual liberty and license, then it is the religious beliefs that must give way and be driven out of American life and culture.

Although American liberty began with the cry of "No King but King Jesus," our nation has now begun to view sexual or erotic expression, rather than religious expression, as our national god and our chief national freedom. It is no longer possible to criticize any chosen sexual lifestyle—even, or perhaps particularly, from a religious or Biblical perspective. Courts preserve abortion as an important means of being able to continue a licentious erotic lifestyle without the accompanying foundational notion of the sacredness of life, family, and fidelity, as God intended within the marital relationship between a man and a woman. While advocates of "anything goes sexually" argue that the Constitution mentions nothing about marriage, it seems obvious that America's founders did not find such a mention necessary when the Judeo-Christian scriptures, as well as thousands of years of culture and history, made the definition of marriage one of those "self-evident" truths mentioned in the Declaration of Independence that were facts of nature and of the Law of Nature that were understood by all human beings without the need for additional reason or further proof.

Those in the activist LGBT community now argue that the "separation of church and state" requires churches and other religious groups and individuals to conform to a new cultural mentality that requires freedom of sexual or erotic expression for all, rather than America's foundational freedom of religious expression. Since *Obergefell*, while Americans may continue to practice the "freedom of worship" and the freedom to hold their religious views in private, they must now conform in the public square to the new cultural norm and the new "foundational" freedom of sexual expression. The Supreme Court's installation of same-sex "marriage" as law removed society's foundational marital institution and replaced religious liberty for all with the hostile and incompatible alternative of licentiousness for all. By redefining marriage, the Court discarded the foundational archetype of civilization, anchored in law, of the created male-female binary on which the continued propagation of the human race depends.

Pro-abortion proponents argue that churches and religious citizens who do not support the killing of unborn children must give way to the cultural notion that unborn children are not really people. This is similar to arguments made in the 18th century that African slaves were not really people either. It took several generations for Christian Americans who truly believed the phrase from the Declaration of Independence that God had created all men equal, to overcome that racist notion. So far nearly 50 years have passed, and we have seen the deaths of tens of millions of unborn babies, and yet America still has not returned to that other original notion found in the Declaration of Independence that the Creator God has endowed all of humanity with the unalienable Right to Life, as well as to Liberty and the Pursuit of Happiness.

Life is now being challenged at both ends of the spectrum—through abortion at the beginning and euthanasia or assisted suicide at the end. In the 21st century our now increasingly paganized culture is even expanding the notion that only certain lives are sacred. Movements now exist to rid America of the old, the sick, and the disabled, as well as the unwanted unborn. This destruction of the unborn, the old, and the disabled is now considered a foundational freedom to choose, while the freedom for certain religious citizens to choose to live out their religious choices in the public square is simultaneously being eroded.

The Demand for Societal Conformity

Logically following on the victories of abortion, euthanasia, and same-sex marriage has been the revision of historic governmental policies that are now being required to conform to the new principle of a fluid gender identity, no matter what science and rationality continue to dictate biologically. The notion of transgenderism now demands a new and complete societal conformity to gender fluidity. Birth certificates must be redefined to reflect that change. Our public schools must permit even children to choose their own gender. It has become a crime in California to use the wrong gender pronoun. No notion of religious liberty can be permitted to interfere with the new legal requirement that everyone must recognize the freedom of choice of gender, despite the Biblical notion that God created mankind biologically as male and female.

Christians, in this modern America, are no longer legally permitted to act on what the Bible teaches—at least not in public.

Instead, the loss of religious liberty now often requires them to believe what 21st century social justice warriors will allow them to believe—at least if they want to teach in public schools, work in certain industries, or operate private businesses linked to wedding services. While many Christians continue to believe the Bible is the Word of God, and the Word of God declares that sexual intimacy is reserved for the lifelong union of a man and a woman in marriage, that all life is sacred, and that gender is assigned by the Creator God, these religious notions may no longer be expressed in public without legal penalty.

This requirement of conformity to certain political views is the underlying reason for the 21st century collapse of religious liberty. No longer does freedom of religious expression protect the right to protest a new American orthodoxy that worships the god of sex and the new foundational right to freedom of sexual expression. Each individual must be permitted to practice the new constitutional right to "define one's own concept of existence, of meaning, of the universe, and of the mystery of human life"—as articulated in *Casey*'s mystery passage—unless "one's concept" is based on the Judeo-Christian religion. No religious opposition to this new government and culturally imposed thinking may be tolerated—all in the name of individualized liberty. But today this liberty only exists, publically at least, for those who toe the new totalitarian line. Is that really the sort of liberty the Pilgrims came to Plymouth Rock to establish?

There now appears to be a death struggle going on in America between those who still believe in America's foundation in the Judeo-Christian religion and those who believe that particular cultural views completely devoid of God or any religious influence must dominate society and government. Americans must now be forced to conform to a new norm of sexual freedom as our ultimate "god-given" liberty, rather than the freedom to perform our religious duties to the Creator God as we see fit.

Statistics Tell A Story

A 2017 report on religious liberty, created by a team of researchers at First Liberty Institute, found that between 2011 and 2016, attacks on religious liberty in America have increased by 133 percent—from 600 cases in 2011 to over 1,400 by 2016. And the severity of the attacks, particularly on Christian beliefs, has gotten worse. Significantly, this study only includes the fraction of religious liberty cases that actually get reported and published. The study also reports a 15 percent increase in attacks on religious liberty just in 2016 alone.

This report provides statistical support to show that Americans have increasingly had their religious liberty rights infringed or "attacked" in one way or another—either in the public arena, in the military, in public schools, or even within church walls. The report concludes: "To deny that religious freedom is in crisis in America is to deny the obvious."

Justin Butterfield, editor of the study and a Harvard law graduate, said his researchers specifically looked for instances where someone was illegally restricted from, or prosecuted for, practicing his or her faith. The report divides cases into four categories: attacks on religion in public areas and in the workplace; attacks on religion in schools; attacks on religion in churches and ministries; and attacks on religion in the military.

Butterfield's research began in 2004, when religious liberty organizations testified during a Senate hearing on discrimination and intolerance based on religion. Two Senators, the late Edward Kennedy (D-MA) and John Cornyn (R-TX), wanted to know how prevalent this issue was.

The results of this study show that, while atheists continue to claim that Christians force their religion on others, it is actually the atheists themselves who have been forcing atheistic secularism on America's students, military personnel, governmental groups, and even private employees and private businesses. Atheists are now seeking to force all Americans to adhere to their lack of belief standards or suffer legal consequences. Far from wanting to "coexist" with those whose beliefs differ from theirs, atheists, pro-abortion advocates, and the activist LGBT community are seeking nothing less than to persecute and ban from the public square all viewpoints that do not conform to their own. Their unrelenting desire is to "convert" the rest of America to their views.

Rev. Barry Lynn, founder of one anti-religious legal organization—Americans United for the Separation of Church and State, went so far as to object to FEMA (the Federal Emergency Management Agency) providing funds for Christian groups that assisted victims of Hurricane Harvey in Texas. His public statement was stunning in its contempt for religion and its heartless attitude toward the victims these Christian groups were assisting. Rev. Lynn said, "We know a lot of people in Texas are suffering, and we are sympathetic. But the fact that something bad has happened does not justify a second wrong. Taxpayers should not be forced to protect religious institutions that they don't subscribe to." Therefore, Christian relief groups, according to Rev. Lynn, should not be entitled to the same government funding as secular groups.

The ultimate irony of this sort of anti-religious secularist position is that these anti-Christian groups are not themselves willing to provide the same relief they seek to prevent churches from providing to disaster victims. Research by the American Enterprise Institute has demonstrated that religious people in America are far more charitable than nonreligious people. Years of research have never shown a measurable way in which secularists are ever demonstrably more charitable than religious people.

When seeking to help those in need, Christians act on a moral imperative of their faith, which requires that they serve Christ by feeding the hungry, clothing the naked, and giving drink to the thirsty. It was Christ Himself who declared, *"Verily, I say unto you, Inasmuch as ye have done it unto one of the least of these my brethren, ye have done it unto me"* (Matt. 25:40 KJV). No such religious beliefs drive the atheist and anti-Christian groups to provide compassionate aid.

The New Public Orthodoxy in America's Schools

Today, instead of being taught valuable and compassionate Judeo-Christian beliefs, America's school children are now being taught to honor the new god of sexual liberty, rather than the Biblical Creator God of America's founders. The new prevailing public orthodoxy is that religious folks, and particularly some Christian sects, are bigots, racists, and extremists.

This is no way to continue the freedom of religious expression, or of any valued American liberty, into the next generation of America's leaders. In addition, in accordance with America's new notions of sex as god, rather than the God of the Bible, our children are being stripped of all semblances of modesty and privacy. Instead, privacy is seen only as a constitutional right that allows abortion, assisted suicide, and sexual license. The concept of modesty is being presented to our children as something old-fashioned that is no longer a virtue. If children object to changing in a locker room with those who reject their own biological gender, it is the children who object who are punished, as a court case from Boyertown, Pennsylvania, demonstrates. Some scientists are now seriously looking into the concept that drugs might be the future answer for "treating" citizens who refuse to conform to the new cultural norms—much as citizens in the Communist Soviet Union who resisted the ideology of the state were treated in mental hospitals and reeducation camps.

Our college students now protest the speech of anyone who wants to come onto their campuses to express an idea in opposition to their non-constitutional view of liberty, which includes the notion of free speech only for those who agree with progressive liberalism. They argue that because contrary speech offends and upsets them, it should not be allowed. This is totally opposite of the principle our courts promoted until the 21st century, which is that the answer to speech with which you disagree is more speech, not censorship.

Speech that disagrees with America's newly evolving culture is now seen as hurtful speech, bullying, or bigoted, rather than as a means of dialogue to arrive at the best cultural attitudes and beliefs.

Another survey, published by the Public Religion Research Institute (PRRI), of more than 100,000 Americans across the nation, found that the number of those who call themselves "religious and spiritual" has declined in America from 59 percent in 2012 to 48 percent in 2017. Currently, just 43 percent of white Americans claim to be Christians. In 1976, that number was 81 percent Christian. That is clearly a significant drop in one generation.

PRRI found that this decline in religious observance and identity is highest in younger Americans. The non-religious or "nones" now make up 34 percent of all Americans under the age of 30. And young Americans who continue to identify as religious and Christian are a shrinking percentage. However, among religiously unaffiliated "none" Americans, only a minority (27 percent) claim to be either agnostic or atheist. Interestingly, those Americans who identify as secular and non-religious do not yet seem to be willing to entirely reject religious beliefs.

That fact is encouraging. Perhaps America's foundational values of freedom based upon the Judeo-Christian religion are not yet entirely lost. Perhaps we still have the opportunity, as Dr. Franklin encouraged, "to keep it."

Ending With Hope

The Pilgrims came to America in 1620 *for* religious freedom, not freedom *from* religion. Today, almost 400 years later, the United States has become an increasingly difficult place for a Christian to work, to be educated, and to serve our country in government or in the military. The right to "not be offended" should never outweigh the right to practice one's religion. Ironically, people rarely ask Christians if it offends *them* to have their child told in school that he cannot pray or that he must shower in the locker room with a child who is biologically of the opposite sex.

It may be hard work in the future to ensure that American Christians continue to have the same constitutional right to express publicly their belief in God as atheists have to publicly express their belief in nothing. But the modern assault on religious liberty can only gain a permanent victory if people of faith choose fear over courage. As President Ronald Reagan said, "Evil is powerless if the good are unafraid." While courage may cost social standing, job mobility, or favor among others, ultimately standing tall in the face of evil gives others courage and reminds us all to do the right thing, despite the consequences.

To end this discussion on the state of religious liberty in America on a positive note, there are some encouraging signs that the decline of religious liberty may itself be on the decline. It will take work and commitment on the part of Christians and others who love liberty to reclaim our original American heritage as it has been expanded and improved as the nation has matured. But that reclamation is not impossible. We have not yet reached a tipping point where liberty is completely gone. But that tipping point may be close. Americans who love liberty cannot sit this one out. We must roll up our sleeves and get to work—quickly.

We continue to have freedom—including religious liberty—today in America, but God has not given us, or any nation, any guarantees. Our second president, John Adams (again), gave a solemn admonition to us, his posterity, in a April 26, 1777, letter to his wife, Abigail. This is a word from his heart that must be taken seriously in the 21st century:

> Posterity! You will never know how much it cost the present generation to preserve your freedom! I hope you will make good use of it! If you do not, I shall repent it in Heaven that I ever took half the pains to preserve it!

There is one very hopeful sign that at least some of President Adams' posterity are still interested in preserving religious freedom. In October 2017, President Donald Trump took an important step to preserve the free exercise of religion by issuing two Department of Justice (DOJ) memoranda to all administrative agencies and executive departments. These memoranda identify 20 key principles of religious liberty and remind government agencies of their obligations under federal law to protect religious liberty in all aspects of their work, including as employers, rule-makers, adjudicators, contract- and grant-makers and program administrators.

The 20 key religious liberty principles identified by President Trump and his DOJ are:

1. The freedom of religion is a fundamental right of paramount importance, expressly protected by federal law.

2. The free exercise of religion includes the right to act or abstain from action in accordance with one's religious beliefs.

3. The freedom of religion extends to persons and organizations.

4. Americans do not give up their freedom of religion by participating in the marketplace, partaking of the public square, or interacting with government.

5. Government may not restrict acts or abstentions because of the beliefs they display.

6. Government may not target religious individuals or entities for special disabilities based on their religion.

7. Government may not target religious individuals or entities through discriminatory enforcement of neutral, generally applicable laws.

8. Government may not officially favor or disfavor particular religious groups.

9. Government may not interfere with the autonomy of a religious organization.

10. The Religious Freedom Restoration Act of 1993 (RFRA) prohibits the federal government from substantially burdening any aspect of religious observance or practice, unless imposition of that burden on a particular religious adherent satisfies strict scrutiny.

11. RFRA's protection extends not just to individuals, but also to organizations, associations, and at least some for-profit corporations.

12. RFRA does not permit the federal government to second-guess the reasonableness of a religious belief.

13. A governmental action substantially burdens an exercise of religion under RFRA if it bans an aspect of an adherent's religious observance or practice, compels an act inconsistent with that observance or practice, or substantially pressures the adherent to modify such observance or practice.

14. The strict scrutiny standard applicable to RFRA is exceptionally demanding.

15. RFRA applies even where a religious adherent seeks an exemption from a legal obligation requiring the adherent to confer benefits on third parties.

16. Title VII of the Civil Rights Act of 1964, as amended, prohibits covered employers from discriminating against individuals on the basis of their religion.

17. Title VII's protection extends to discrimination on the basis of religious observance or practice as well as belief, unless the employer cannot reasonably accommodate such observance or practice without undue hardship on the business.

18. The Clinton Guidelines on Religious Exercise and Religious Expression in the Federal Workplace provide useful examples for private employers of reasonable accommodations for religious observance and practice in the workplace.

19. Religious employers are entitled to employ only persons whose beliefs and conduct are consistent with the employers' religious precepts.

20. As a general matter, the federal government may not condition receipt of a federal grant or contract on the effective relinquishment of a religious organization's exemptions or attributes of its religious character.

In addition, the Trump Administration's Department of Justice, earlier in 2017, demonstrated a shift in policy from the Obama Administration by commenting in the case of *Zarda v. Altitude Express* that Title VII of the Civil Rights Act of 1964 bans gender discrimination in the workplace; however, that law does not automatically include sexual orientation or gender identity.

This list from the 2017 Presidential Memoranda provides an outline of the field where the battle for religious liberty is being waged, but is does not ensure that the battle is won. Time may be short. It is difficult to say just how much longer we will retain the opportunity to make a real change in our government and culture. American Christians must become informed about the Biblical principles that ordered the founding of this great nation and we must continue to follow those principles if we are to survive as a free people. May God grant us grace and courage for the task.

CHAPTER 6

The Bible and Life*

by D. James Kennedy and Jerry Newcombe

I call heaven and earth to witness against you today, that I have set before you life and death, blessing and curse. Therefore choose life, that you and your offspring may live.
DEUTERONOMY 30:19

Is human life cheap? It depends on which worldview prevails—the Christian one that sees man made in God's image, or the pagan one that sees us as the product of time, plus chance, plus impersonal forces of nature.

Read the papers today, and you are liable to come across some new, grisly story. I remember hearing about a vicious crime a few years ago—and there have been many—when a group of young teenagers in America stabbed an immigrant ice-cream truck driver. The poor man was just trying to make a living in his newly-adopted country. Instead, he got stabbed by inner-city toughs, who danced around him as he writhed on the ground, slowing dying, while the teens helped themselves to ice cream bars and other goodies from his truck.

How cheap has human life become?

Life has, indeed, become cheap in modern America. This has

many manifestations: abortion, infanticide, the push for cloning and destroying embryonic stem cells for their body parts, homicide, suicide, and euthanasia.

Think about all the gratuitous violence Hollywood pumps out or the rappers celebrate. Inner-city life in many places in this country approximates a war zone. Why has life been so cheapened? We believe there are several factors to this, but, without a doubt, one of them is abortion. As Mother Teresa so pointedly asked years ago, "And if we accept that a **mother** can kill **her own child,** how can we tell others not to kill?" [Emphasis added.][1] It's a great question.

Consider the example of our modern rappers. Usher became the number one rapper of 2004. There was a remix of his song "Confessions" by rapper Joe Budden. This remix includes a scenario where one fellow tells his girlfriend that if she's pregnant, she'd better abort it. Otherwise, he'd deliver a powerful blow to her stomach to make sure it's "leakin."[2] This is how cheap human life has become in some parts of our culture—assault and abortion are celebrated in what purports to be entertainment.

Father John Powell once said that when a woman has an abortion, she either becomes guilty or hard—as in hardhearted. That's a great insight. While millions of women who are "post-abortive" suffer in silence, there are millions of others who celebrate abortion as if it's a good thing.

Even the most pro-abortion rights person will admit that having an abortion is difficult and gut-wrenching. Have we gotten so calloused about such a sensitive issue? Indeed, some people try to make it so accepted by trivializing it. An example of this is the poem by Theo Kogan on the website *PunkVoter.com.*

> As a person and as a woman I value my freedom,
> whether its the freedom to speak out,
>
> • to look the way I want,

- live the way I want, create art and music,

- choosing what I want to do with my body,

- whether it's my hair color,

- tattoos, piercing,

- squeezing a zit,

- plucking a hair or having an abortion.[3]

So, in other words, aborting your unborn child is no more consequential than pulling an unwanted hair. How callous can we be?

Also in 2004, Planned Parenthood came out with a new T-shirt, which had emblazoned on it the proclamation that I'm sure girls and ladies were proud to tell the world: "I had an abortion."[4] As we get further away from God, life becomes cheaper and cheaper. Yet, even many professing Christians have a sub-Christian view of human life.

In the Image of God

The starting point of all discussions about the value of human life from a Biblical perspective can be found in the book of Genesis. *So God created man in his own image, in the image of God he created him; male and female he created them* (Genesis 1:27).

That we are made in God's own image has become a cliché. Therefore, it has lost some of its punch. But this is a radical concept. The implications that flow from this starting point—how we view the value of man—are immense and immeasurable.

Consider the issue of abortion in the light of this well-known passage from the Psalms: *For you formed my inward parts; you knitted me together in my mother's womb. I praise you, for I am fearfully and wonderfully made* (Psalm 139:13-14).

If this isn't a strong declaration for the unborn child, for the rights of the "fetus" (which is simply Latin for "unborn child"), I don't know what is.

Jeremiah also reiterates the theme of God doing something for him while he was yet in the womb. *"Before I formed you in the womb I knew you, and before you were born I consecrated you"* (Jeremiah 1:5). God doesn't consecrate blobs of tissue—but people.

In the gospel of Luke, we read the account of when Elizabeth was pregnant with John the Baptist, and her cousin Mary, who was bearing Jesus, came to visit. When the two greeted each other, the baby in Elizabeth's womb leaped for joy. "Things" don't have joy.

Elizabeth said, "The baby in my womb leaped for joy." You never hear a woman say that the fetus inside her leaped for joy. It is always the "baby." The Greek word for baby is *brephos;* the baby in the womb is the *brephos*. What does that mean? It is the same term that was used to describe Jesus to the shepherds: "You will find a baby wrapped in swaddling cloths and lying in a manger." That is a baby—not a tumor—but a baby.

Sanctity of Life Versus the "Quality of Life"

Cal Thomas has said, "Abortion is the most volatile issue that has faced America since the civil war."[5] The abortion decision changed how Americans look at human life. It substituted the pagan-humanistic view—the "quality of life ethic"—for the Judeo-Christian based view of the sanctity of life.

At the heart of this conflict is a battle between worldviews. Is human life just the product of time plus chance, or are we uniquely made in the image of God? There is a great clash in our country between the concept of *sanctity* of life and the concept of *quality* of life. People have heard and read many such discussions, and I am afraid that for most, they do not grasp the full implication of what that means.

The concept of 'sanctity of life' is a spiritual concept; it is a religious concept. The word "sanctity" which comes from the Latin word *sanctitas* from *sanctus,* means holy or sacred unto

God, inviolable, that which God has declared is of great value. It is, therefore, a spiritual concept.

However, for a humanist or an atheist or an unbeliever of most any kind, there is no such thing as "sanctity of life." Unless there is a God who has given us a spirit and who sanctifies us, there cannot be a sanctity-of-life ethic.

'Quality of life' is a physical concept. There is no one who can look at another and determine the quality of his soul. If life is merely molecules in motion, then we can have a quality-of-life ethic. But if we are Christians and believe that there is an infinite, eternal, and unchangeable God who is a Spirit, who has given to us everlasting spirits, and if we have an inalienable right to life, then we cannot accept a "quality of life" ethic.

Here is the conflict in brutal simplicity: the Judeo-Christian concept of life vs. the humanistic, evolutionary view. The humanists may pride themselves at their creation of a new man, but make no mistake—take their perspective to the nth degree and you have one group of people deciding on whether others should be able to live or die. Perhaps, the battleground where this clash of worldviews is the hottest today is in the abortion chambers across the land.

Our belief about origins impacts everything else, including whether we place any value on human life. Are we just the product of time plus chance and random forces? Or are we the unique creation of God? How we answer that question is the difference ultimately between Auschwitz and Austria.

The astrophysicist Carl Sagan said that there is and never has been anything in the universe but "matter." If one has that kind of a totally non-spiritual view, we will have in the quality of life simply a physical understanding of life. Now, we may indeed say that this person has come closer to the perfect ideal of human life than that person ... or this person here ... or that one is somewhat in between. But if every soul has been created by God and has infinite value, then there are no degrees of qualification between the two.

If I may say something radical, let me say: "We hold these truths to be self-evident, that all men are created equal, that they are endowed by their Creator with certain inalienable rights, that among these are Life. . . ." Therefore, it is only from a purely atheistic, humanistic, secularistic view that one can determine that a life is to be valued, depending solely upon the physical characteristics of that life.

The Slippery Slope

Some of our modern courts have rendered decisions on life and death. They have taken us another step down that "slippery slope"—the courts having already decided that it is legal to let a person die. There is a great difference between letting a person die naturally and causing him to die by starvation. I would agree that we need not go to heroic mechanical means of keeping a person alive for many, many years when he simply has machines breathing for him and making his heart beat, and he really is not "alive." The person may or may not die in the near future, if he is allowed to do so naturally, but he will most certainly die if food and water are removed. He is then made to die slowly.

Let me say, my friend, it is a very, very short step between making a person die by starvation and making them die by a legal and lethal injection of poison. In fact, when philosopher Dr. Helga Kuhse, spoke to 500 participants at a euthanasia conference she said, "Once you show them how painful it is to starve to death, they will [gladly] accept lethal injections." That is a very small step down that slope.

Outside of Atlanta is the famous Stone Mountain. Perhaps you have been there and even have climbed it. If you go there, you will notice a long, slow incline to the top of the mountain. From there, it begins to gradually decline for about a hundred feet and then falls off precipitously hundreds of feet to the ground below. Back at the top is a rope barrier to keep people from going down that very long and very gradual decline. Those who ignore this warning tend to go out just a little bit farther to get a better look over the edge. Before they realize it, their feet are slipping and sliding. Then they plunge off into the air and land hundreds of feet below. Many people have fallen off that mountain and died as a result. It is that slippery slope that leads to the precipice and to death. Today our society is right now a good way down that slope.

Dr. C. Everett Koop, former Surgeon General, said there is something that the abortionists, the infanticide promoters, and the euthanasia proponents always do: they take a few extreme examples and use these to gain sympathy for ideas and practices that later are not limited to extreme cases. To wit: What have we heard about abortion? The poor girl who is the victim of rape or is the victim of incest—surely, you're going to allow that. Using such examples over and over again, they have succeeded in making abortion legal. Now close to 60 million American babies have been killed, less than two percent of which had anything to do with rape or incest. The same thing is now happening with euthanasia and infanticide.

"An Act of Raw Judicial Power"

In 1973, when the judges of the Supreme Court of the United States again demonstrated their "consummate" wisdom by their decision in *Roe v. Wade,* they said that unborn children are not "persons," and therefore, are not deserving of the protection of our Constitution and our laws. Thus, the American holocaust was unleashed.

Today those aborted babies would be out in the work force, rearing children and changing our world. Many of them would be graduating from high school and choosing colleges, but one out of every four of their age group is not here. If you watched a graduation ceremony this past year, you should know that every fourth place should have been held by an empty cap and gown for that child who was not there— not there to be valedictorian, not there to become a doctor, lawyer, minister, or perhaps even president of the United States. Almost sixty million Americans are missing in this bloody action that has been such a dark blotch on the escutcheon of our country.

We should never forget that when the decision in *Roe v. Wade* came down, not all the Supreme Court justices agreed with it. Justice Byron White, who was appointed by President John F. Kennedy, dissented on the decision and called it "an act of raw judicial power."[6] Justice William Rehnquist (who was promoted to be the Chief Justice in the mid-1980s) also dissented.

The *Roe v. Wade* decision purports to be based on the Constitution. What provisions of the constitution were cited to make the case? Where do we find the right for a woman to "terminate a pregnancy"? Where do we find the "right to privacy"? We don't.

Here are the two portions of the Constitution that are cited as the "constitutional basis" for *Roe v. Wade*:

- Amendment IX: The enumeration in the Constitution, of certain rights, shall not be construed to deny or disparage others retained by the people.

- Amendment XIV, SECTION 1: All persons born or naturalized in the United States, and subject to the jurisdiction thereof, are citizens of the United States and of the State wherein they reside. No state shall make or enforce any law which shall abridge the privileges or immunities of citizens of the United States; nor shall any State deprive any person of life, liberty, or property, without due process of law; nor deny to any person within its jurisdiction the equal protection of the laws.

So where exactly is the provision in the Constitution that gives them the right to kill the unborn? Michael Farris is a constitutional attorney and the CEO of Alliance Defending Freedom. He has this to say about the "constitutional" basis of decisions like *Roe v. Wade*: "They're just making this stuff up! Show me the amendment. Show me the language. Show me the textual provision, and then maybe

I'll agree with you. But until then, it's just thin air. It's smoke and mirrors. It's a shell game with our Constitution."[7]

Interestingly, Roe herself (Norma McCorvey) disagreed with *Roe v. Wade*. The late Norma McCorvey[8] became a Christian and was thoroughly pro-life and even attempted to correct the terrible legal precedent her case caused. Norma documented her story in her book, *Won by Love*.[9]

Part of what made the U.S. Supreme Court's decision in *Roe v. Wade* so bad is that it converts physicians from healers to killers. Dr. William J. Brennan, professor at St. Louis University, points out just how scary this shift is:

> The perversion of medicine in the service of killing is accompanied by a redefinition of barbaric acts as valid medical procedures. An astounding bit of alchemy sets in whereby the physician-healer not only becomes a killer, but in the process of this most radical of transformations, destruction loses its most repulsive features and becomes incorporated into the fabric of respectable medical practice.[10]

How Abortions Are Performed

As Dr. Brennan stated, we have now redefined "barbaric acts as valid medical procedures," and although it is painful to consider, we should understand just how barbaric these procedures truly are.

One of the most common types of abortion uses a high-powered vacuum cleaner to suck out the unborn baby, piece by piece, chunk by chunk. In another type of abortion, the abortionist reaches into the womb with forceps to rip off a leg, then another leg, then an arm—all while the baby may still be alive and fighting to avoid the forceps. Then the abortionist rips off the other arm and reaches in to crush the baby's head so the dead baby can be pulled out of its mother's womb.

These procedures are performed in the first and second trimester of gestation. But some women come seeking abortions even in the third trimester. To accommodate late-term abortions, some doctors started doing "partial-birth abortions." In this procedure the abortionist would move the baby into a breach birth position and pull out the baby's feet, and then the rest of the body—everything but the head. Understandably, the baby would be writhing in pain; then the doctor would puncture the back of the base of the baby's skull with scissors and put a tube into the baby's skull and suck out the baby's brains. When the skull was largely empty, the abortionist would pull what's left of the baby's head out of the womb.

For a number of years there was a battle over this barbaric procedure of partial-birth abortion in Congress and the U.S. Supreme Court. In fact, three times Congress voted to ban it. However, former President Clinton vetoed the ban twice. Finally, in 2003, Congress passed a ban a third time, and this time President Bush signed it into law. Tragically, within hours, the ACLU and their fellow travelers filed suit, effectively blocking the law, tying it up in court. Finally, in 2007, the U.S. Supreme Court upheld the ban with their decision in *Gonzales v. Carhart.*

Since then, however, abortionists have not stopped their barbaric practices. A different method for doing late-term abortions as late as 35 weeks has been developed that takes 3-4 days to complete. The abortionist first injects Digoxin or potassium chloride into the baby's heart or the amniotic fluid in the mother's womb. This gives the baby a fatal heart attack. After the Digoxin injection, the woman's cervix is packed with thin tampon-like sticks made of seaweed called "laminaria," which are used to expand the cervix gradually over the next day. The drug Misoprostol is also administered vaginally to prepare the cervix for the upcoming delivery of the dead baby and stimulate contractions.

After the first day's injection, the woman is sent home or to a local hotel to wait for her next appointment at the abortion facility the following day. She is not monitored by any medical personnel during this time. The next day, she is given more Misoprostol and larger laminaria sticks are inserted, after which she is again sent away without anyone to assist her, until she returns the final day to deliver her dead baby.

Sometimes women can't reach the abortion facility in time and will deliver their dead babies in the hotel, in a vehicle, or another place where there is no medical assistance available.[11]

Every abortion, no matter how old the fetus is, ends up with a dead baby.

The media knows that if any of these things were shown on television, this horror would come to an end. The Bible says that the Lord hates those who shed innocent blood (Prov. 6:16-17). And I say woe unto those people who have complicity in it.

Just think about the complicity of the media. It is virtually impossible to get any television station in America to show a picture of an aborted child, but how many tens of thousands of victims of the Nazi holocaust have been shown on television? How many pictures of slaves in productions like Roots have been shown on television? How many times did we see the burnt bodies of people from the Vietnam War brought right into our living room? Yet, never a picture of an aborted child, because abortion proponents know that if the light were shined in that darkness, abortion would end.

"If Wombs Had Windows"

Shari Richard, a sonographer who takes sonograms of babies in the womb, said something I think is very, very perceptive: "If wombs had windows, abortion would end." Think about it. If the light was shone into that darkness, people would see the atrocities and they would recoil in horror and demand, "This must end. How could people allow such a thing to happen?" Unfortunately, abortion happens in secrecy behind the well-protected doors of abortion clinics and behind the walls of the mother's womb, unseen and unheard.

As the former owner of a number of abortion facilities, Carol Everett has first-hand knowledge of the deception at the heart of the abortion industry. She says, "In the front counseling room, the young woman is asking, 'Is it a baby?' And she's being told, 'No.' But in the back, every single baby, as early as it can be done, has to be put back together—arms, legs, hands, feet, the head, and the spine—to be sure it's all there. It is a baby."[12]

So we have semantic deception: "Not a person . . . It's something else . . . It's a blob of tissue . . . " Or "It's P.O.C., 'products of conception.'" Some clinics have even told women the fetus appears to have gill slits in various stages of development. They tell a young lady, "You see, it's just a fish. We kill fish, don't we?" Yet, these indentations are not gill slits and have nothing to do with fish; they never connect to the lungs. These marks eventually produce the ears and other glands in the neck, but some clinics have deceived people into believing the fetus is a fish-like evolutionary ancestor. And so the deception goes on.

The Right to Life Is the Most Basic Right

In one of Dr. Francis Schaeffer's last messages, he said that the right to life is more fundamental and basic than the right of liberty or the pursuit of happiness, or any other right, for that matter. Indeed, if you are lying in your coffin, you do not care how many shackles and chains have been wrapped around you to restrict your freedom. Nor do you care how much money you have in your bank account. Without life, nothing else really matters. The baby in the womb has as much of a right to life as any of us.

Today the word "choice" has been distorted to mean death. In the Old Testament, God spoke to His people through Moses about choice. He said, "Choose life." What this really meant was that by choosing Him, they were choosing life. This is something we believe God would say to America today: "Choose life."

What choice do the abortionists give these women? One man who is head of a pro-life organization was picketing an abortion facility.

When the facility's manager told this man to stop picketing, he said, "Give me a small desk in an obscure corner, and just a few minutes to talk to each of the women to simply present the adoption option and explain to them what it is they are carrying in their womb, and I will call off the pickets."

The manager replied, "Over my dead body."

Pro-choice indeed! The only "choice" the abortionists ever give anybody is "Tuesday or Friday? When do you want to have the abortion?" Any of you who may be pro-choice, I just want to say this to you: "You ought to get down on your knees and thank God that your mother wasn't pro-choice."

This reminds me of a quip from Ronald Reagan. During one of the 1980 presidential debates between him and Jimmy Carter, he was asked by a reporter why he did not support the pro-choice position. In his characteristic folksy manner, the future president declared, "Well, I happen to notice that everyone who is pro-choice has already been born."

Some people say, "Well, I'm personally opposed to abortion, but I can't impose my values on other people." Wait a minute, suppose Abraham Lincoln had had that view as president. "My fellow Americans, I am personally opposed to slavery and would never own a slave," he would have said. "However, I cannot impose my values on others. If others choose to own slaves, that, of course, is their prerogative."

I can assure you of one thing: if that had been the case, we would rarely hear of Abraham Lincoln. Instead, he is considered the greatest and most famous of all American presidents, precisely because he took a firm, moral stand for that which was right.

Christian Responses to Abortion

Just as people today have asked, "What were the German Christians doing when the Nazis were slaughtering Jews?" our grandchildren may ask, "What were you doing during the American holocaust? Why did you not stop it?" Someday the mask of silence and secrecy and darkness will be taken away, and everyone will see all the ghastly details. Then they will say, "How could you have lived during all of that and never lifted a hand or your voice to stop it?"

A Christian world-and-life view is opposed to abortion. This is why Christians go out of their way to help provide an alternative for unwed mothers so they don't go that route. That is why Christians provide counseling and healing for those—including professing Christians—who have had abortions. There is forgiveness for all sins when we repent and call on Jesus.

You certainly can find all types at a public rally. You can also find all sorts of strange signs. Co-author Jerry Newcombe went to a massive pro-life rally in Washington, D.C. many years ago and will never forget one of those signs from that rally. A young man held high a handmade poster proclaiming: "Former Fetuses, Unite!" It may seem comical. It may seem so obvious, but it's true: we're all former fetuses.

Isn't it time we unite to protect the most vulnerable amongst us? I believe a Christian world and life view will always honor and cherish life. That is why from the beginning of the church to the very present day, Christians have worked hard to provide for the orphans (and the widows, too) and to protect the life of the unborn. It goes back to the simple Christian worldview: God is the giver and taker of life. It is not up to us to take life, only to care for it.

* Adapted in part from *Lord of All: Developing a Christian World-and-Life View* (Crossway Books, 2005)

CHAPTER 7

The Incarceration of America

by Linda W. Smith

. . . a bruised reed he will not break, and a faintly burning wick
he will not quench; he will faithfully bring forth justice.
ISAIAH 42:3

"Equal Justice Under Law" are the words written above the entrance to the U.S. Supreme Court. One of the unique aspects of the American experiment was the guarantee given of justice. But what has happened to justice in America? We have become a nation that has incarcerated its citizens at an unprecedented rate. In the United States, 700 out of every 100,000 people are in prison or jail. This is the highest incarceration rate, by far, anywhere in the world, with the closest competitor being Australia with a rate of 152 in 100,000.[1]

How Did We Get Here?

The explanation for this incredible rate of incarceration can be laid at the feet of our welfare policies beginning in the 1930s. These policies came from a misinterpretation of so-called social justice by liberal policy makers. Because of the policies implemented to take care of the poor and disadvantaged in an unBiblical way, we have reaped the unintended and untoward consequences of instilling in many recipients a disincentive to work, resulting in a sense of hopelessness and uselessness leading to negative behavior. This chapter will trace how the United States got to the point where we have become a "culture of incarceration," beginning with our welfare policies based on a liberal social justice interpretation. These policies have resulted in increases in unwed mothers, absentee fathers, abortion, substance abuse, a lack of a work ethic and education and training, and, ultimately, generational crime and a higher rate of incarceration of our citizens.

God Designed Us to Work

We read in Genesis that God gave man "jobs" when he created him. It is in this work that we gain satisfaction and a sense of purpose. God gave us both physical and intellectual work to provide a balance in our lives—one was not superior to the other.

The welfare system gave a disincentive to working. When man moves to areas not designed by his Creator, we reap the disorder we are in today. God designed man, and He knows what he needs. Scripture clearly bears out our design for the need to work in Genesis 1:26, 28; Genesis 2:15, 19-20; and Ecclesiastes 3:22.

I saw the negative impact of our welfare system subverting His plan for us up close and personal when I was working in a very poor rural area near Elkins, West Virginia, conducting a household interview survey. Unrelated to the questionnaire, I asked one of the children, who was around 12 years old, what he planned to do when he grew up. He looked very perplexed at the question, so I restated it to ask him what job he wanted to do when he grew up. His response was astonishing. "I'm gonna go on welfare like my daddy" was the young man's reply. That response has never left me. To think that government handouts had given him no hope of a better life than to live in such poverty, no incentive to do better, to achieve more, or to get a better education was one of the most disheartening things I have ever experienced.

The Liberal View of Social Justice

The liberal view of social justice is the need for redistribution of wealth and resources, claiming unfair treatment of certain groups based on various factors—including race, gender, education, healthcare, and culture.

They note the need for social justice is due to social inequality as a result of personal beliefs by some that are discriminatory or by governmental laws and regulations that ultimately discriminate against these groups. As a result, we have adopted policies that ultimately resulted in incarcerating more of our citizens because incentives to work, from which dignity and a sense of purpose flow, have been eliminated and have been replaced with destructive behavior.

The Biblical View of Social Justice

The goal of justice is to increase righteousness.[2] Throughout Scripture we are admonished to take care of the poor and needy and widows and orphans (Isaiah 1:17; Zechariah 7: 9-10), and not to take care of those who will not work when they are capable of doing so (2 Thessalonians 3:10).

Author Marvin Olasky points out that social justice as used "by liberal preachers and journalists is thoroughly unBiblical: Many equate social justice with fighting a free enterprise system that purportedly keeps people poor, but in reality is their best economic hope."[3]

The Biblical view of social justice is best stated by Jesus when He said in Mark 12:20-21 (NIV): "'Love the Lord your God with all your heart and with all your soul and with all your mind and with all your strength.' The second is this: 'Love your neighbor as yourself.' There is *no commandment greater than these.*" We are to do right by everyone based on that person's need. It is not necessarily the government's responsibility to do this. It is up to each of us and to our churches and to charitable organizations to assist those in need. If that requires mentoring, or food, or shelter, or clothing, or visiting them in prison, that is what is to be provided. This is summarized well in Micah 6:8 (NIV): "*He has shown you, O mortal, what is good. And what does the Lord require of you? To act justly and to love mercy and to walk humbly with your God.*"

Helping those in need does not mean redistribution of wealth. It is far greater than that. It is to act righteously toward our fellowman.

We landed in our current welfare situation by a series of perhaps "well-meaning," yet unBiblical "solutions" to the problem. We thought that if we could just give those who were less fortunate some "assistance" they soon would pull themselves up and get jobs and all would be better. But that hasn't happened. The plight of offenders and the fact that the United States incarcerates individuals at a higher rate by far than any other country in the world is a key example of social justice gone haywire. The opposite of what was intended has happened.

The Welfare State

How did welfare begin in the United States?

Throughout history there have been some means to take care of the poor—whether through government programs or through charitable organizations. However, in the United States, during the Great Depression of the 1930s, government programs and charitable organizations could not handle the exorbitant need. These were extremely difficult times when nutrition and healthcare were lacking for many, jobs were lost, and many could not sustain themselves.

President Franklin D. Roosevelt created jobs through his public works programs to assist in getting people back to work. He also endorsed programs to aid children and other dependent groups, and as a result, the United States had a welfare program in place by 1935.

This was an extreme departure from the pride of American workers who placed great significance in their work ethic and saw themselves as self-sufficient.

Certainly, something dramatic needed to be done to assist during this most extraordinary time; the states and charitable organizations could not meet the need when a series of circumstances converged to require extreme measures. However, these measures were kept in place even after the economy turned around, and they were even expanded.

Through the Social Security Act, Roosevelt permanently secured the federal government's responsibility for its citizens.[4]

In his State of the Union Address on January 4, 1935, Franklin D. Roosevelt noted that "In most Nations social justice, no longer a distant ideal, has become a definite goal, and ancient Governments are beginning to heed the call." He also said that we must ensure "the security against the major hazards and vicissitudes of life." Roosevelt explained his goals:

> The lessons of history, confirmed by the evidence immediately before me, show conclusively that continued dependence upon relief induces a spiritual and moral disintegration fundamentally destructive to the national fiber. To dole out relief in this way is to administer a narcotic, a subtle destroyer of the human spirit. It is inimical to the dictates of sound policy. It is in violation of the traditions of America. Work must be found for able-bodied but destitute workers.[5]

So he believed that by providing this new kind of security for citizens that the need for "make work" would go away.

During the next few decades, a number of welfare programs were established, including Medicaid, public housing, and food stamps. Concerns over dependency on welfare began to rise, however, recognizing it as a disincentive to full-time employment. President Lyndon

B. Johnson's Great Society and The War on Poverty had little impact. Speaking of the latter, poverty researcher Michael D. Tanner says:

> Throwing money at the problem has neither reduced poverty nor made the poor self-sufficient. Instead, government programs have torn at the social fabric of the country and been a significant factor in increasing out-of-wedlock births with all of their attendant problems. They have weakened the work ethic and contributed to rising crime rates. Most tragically of all, the pathologies they engender have been passed on from parent to child, from generation to generation.[6]

Tanner also notes "The failures of the War on Poverty should serve as an object lesson for policymakers today. Good intentions are not enough. We should not continue to throw money at failed programs in the name of compassion."[7]

Under President Richard M. Nixon, the number on the welfare rolls continued to rise.

President Ronald Reagan, who was a serious critic of abuses of welfare, was able to secure cuts in some programs.

Researcher Dr. Charles Murray, who has examined welfare practices for decades, argues that welfare actually hurts the poor, making them less well-off and has trapped single parents in it. He recommended abolishing it.[8]

The 1996 welfare reform law, Personal Responsibility and Work Opportunity Reconciliation Act (PRWORA), actually did a good deal of what Murray supported, making "personal responsibility and work central to the welfare agenda, and it shifted welfare to the states."[9]

However, we are still a welfare state. Much change is needed.

A good place to start, as pointed out by The Brookings Institute, is the following: individuals have a 98 percent chance of avoiding poverty if they do three things: 1) graduate high school, 2) work full time, and 3) marry before having children. Only two percent of those who do these things end up in poverty.[10]

Taking God Out of Public Schools

Another event that has contributed to our "culture of incarceration" resulting from a sense of lack of purpose and the ensuing hopelessness was the U.S. Supreme Court's decision in *Engel v. Vitale* on June 25, 1962. In that decision, the court ruled that a prayer approved by the New York Board of Regents for use in schools violated the First Amendment by constituting an "establishment of religion." Then the following year, in *Abington School District v. Schempp*, the Court prohibited Bible readings in public schools for similar reasons.

Writer Michael D. Waggoner notes:

> These two landmark Supreme Court decisions centered on the place of religion in public education, and particularly the place of Protestantism, which had long been accepted as the given American faith tradition. Both decisions ultimately changed the face of American civil society, and in turn, helped usher in the last half-century of the culture wars.[11]

These two court decisions signaled America's turn away from God. In Romans 1:18-25, we read about the chaos and moral disintegration that we have reaped in our culture for refusing to acknowledge God.

Unwed mothers

We see yet another consequence of our erroneous welfare policies in the increase of out of-wedlock births, which have risen

129

steadily since 1940.[12]

Poverty expert Robert Rector of the Heritage Foundation writes:

> . . . when President Lyndon Johnson launched the War on Poverty in 1964, 93 percent of children born in the United States were born to married parents. Since that time, births within marriage have declined sharply. In 2010, only 59 percent of all births in the nation occurred to married couples. . . . When the War on Poverty began in the mid-1960s, only 6 percent of children were born out of wedlock. Over the next four and a half decades, the number rose rapidly. In 2010, 40.8 percent of all children born in the U.S. were born outside of marriage.[13]

Abortion

Then we have the reprehensible *Roe v. Wade* decision on January 22, 1973, when the Supreme Court decriminalized abortion. This, indeed, was America's death knell, starting us down the path to the lack of purpose and hopelessness experienced, in particular by those who are so vulnerable—the poor—as we attack the *most* vulnerable—the unborn. This lack of regard for the unborn has produced a general lack of regard for *any* human life, and it has altered the entire economy of the United States.

Writer Mitch Benna points out:

> According to the Bureau of Labor Statistics, Social Security Administration, Guttmacher Institute, and National Center for Health Statistics, if abortion had never been legalized in 1973, more than 17 million people would be employed, resulting in an additional $400 billion from those workers, with $11 billion contributed to Medicare and $47 million contributed

to Social Security. Although it is important to also reduce government spending, these added incomes would nevertheless help the country.[14]

Steven Ertelt, the founder and director of Lifenews.com, writes, "After almost 40 years of legalized abortions throughout the United States—and longer in states that okayed abortions pre-*Roe*—the U.S. population has been decimated to the point that the nation is seeing the lowest population growth since the 1930s."[15]

Where Do We Go from Here?

What was intended for "good" by the social justice liberals serves only as a means to keep the oppressed down forever and has a devastating impact on our economy. The negative consequences of our welfare state are no more evident than in the case of criminal offenders and our response to them.

Indeed, the current incarceration rate of offenders is having a devastating impact on our country related to: 1) the financial cost of incarceration to the American public,[16] 2) its impact on offenders, and 3) its impact on their families and communities. And, for the most part, it isn't helping! The recidivism rate among the federal prison population is 49.3 percent, with the majority returning to prison within the first two years of release.[17] In large part, we have been ineffective in our response to the crime problem in this country. The trend has been largely to "incarcerate our way out of it"—especially for the populations in our inner cities.[18]

A change in public policy is needed. Our criminal justice problem is a generational problem, and, therefore, we must approach it in this way. We need to re-examine not only our welfare system, but our approach to the incarceration of prisoners by working with their families and communities.

Virtually all prisoners will eventually be released to the community. While in prison, most inmates take part in education or job training programs. However, they are often still ill-prepared to return to a crime-free life and lack a solid release plan. The biggest impediments to success upon release are lack of a marketable skill for the community to which they are released. Also, they return to the same environment that facilitated their criminal behavior in the first place, and they associate with the same crowd as before. The Bible says, "Bad company corrupts good morals." When these negative factors converge, a sense of hopelessness sets in, and ex-offenders often quickly revert to the lifestyle they maintained prior to prison.

Sadly, children of offenders are more likely to be involved themselves in criminal behavior and other destructive behavior. Fifty-two percent of state inmates and 63 percent of federal inmates reported having minor children for a total of 1,706,600 children, accounting for 2.3 percent of the U.S. resident population under age 18.[19] This is a staggering number, especially considering the fact that children of prisoners are about three times as likely as other children to be involved in the criminal justice system.[20] Half of parents in state prison reported they had a family member who had been incarcerated; 39.9 percent of state offenders and 31.2 percent of federal offenders report their family had received some form of public assistance; and 33.7 percent of state offenders and 27.2 percent of federal offenders report a parent or guardian abused drugs or alcohol.[21]

We must do something not only for offenders currently incarcerated, or who will be incarcerated in the near-term, and who will eventually be released to the community, but prospectively for the generation not yet involved in criminal behavior—the children of the inmates and the children of the communities from where they come. We must intervene with these children before the destructive behavior begins. The environment in which they are raised breeds this type of behavior, and if we do not intervene, we will see this vicious cycle continuing.

We must find options and alternatives to what we have been doing because for the most part it is not working. We need to address not only offenders' challenges and difficulties, but those of their families and communities.

There is one caveat to the proposed options presented below. These options should not be considered for individuals with crimes of violence. Indeed, there are crimes so heinous and individuals with such a propensity for violence that nothing but lifelong incarceration (or in some cases, the death penalty) is demanded. And other crimes require incarceration to fulfill the need for retribution and deterrence. Each response must be tailored to the individual.

Options for Consideration (Federal System):

- Re-examine drug offender incarceration. Fifty percent of federal system inmates are confined for drug offenses. All do not need to be incarcerated and certainly not all for lengthy periods of time.

- Reinstate Federal Parole.

- Expand "good time options." If an inmate really does well in prison (learning a marketable skill or completing significant educational programming, and has developed a good work ethic), AND has a solid release plan, substantial good time could be granted. (An independent body such as the federal Parole Commission—if reinstated—would grant this good time.)

- Examine reducing or eliminating mandatory minimum sentences.

- Use more alternatives to incarceration for non-violent offenders.

- Involve local churches in mentoring and assisting inmate families while the offender is incarcerated.

- Involve local churches in mentoring inmates and ex-inmates both pre- and post-release, and form coalitions of local churches to accomplish this.

- Establish boarding schools for children of offenders and those children in the communities from which offenders come, and *offer* parents the opportunity for their children to participate. The cost of this will be offset by future savings by avoiding costs related to the criminal justice and welfare systems, and avoiding the destructive behavior and pain and devastation that would have come to more families and more communities in the future.

It is only through a change in public policy that we can begin to turn around our nation. These prescriptions are specifically related to the "incarceration of America" but true change in the United States must begin with an overhaul of our welfare system based on a Biblical model.

Closing Thought from Chuck Colson

The late Chuck Colson served in the Nixon Administration, and he was one of about 80 men from that group who ended up in jail for Watergate related crimes. Colson hated prison and viewed this as his life's biggest failure. Yet, in prison, as a newly born-again Christian, Colson gained a new calling—to help with prison reform through Christian commitment. He founded Prison Fellowship, which is now active in many nations around the world. It helps prisoners find

Christ and fellowship in prison, and it helps them after the prison program through the use of Christian mentors on the outside—who befriend the inmates on the inside.

In one of our many D. James Kennedy Ministries programs in which Chuck Colson appeared, he made this remark, which helps show how ultimately Jesus is the answer:

> What we have got to understand is that when Christ really comes into a person's life and they're transformed, they can begin to do the right thing. So, our job as Christians is to cultivate a deep relationship with Christ; learn the virtues which He's teaching, get it into our Bible studies, get it into our youth groups.

Colson mentions a prison in Minnesota, which allowed inmates on a voluntary basis to opt into a program of Christian discipleship within the prison through the auspices of Prison Fellowship. Colson noted that the result was:

> . . . that prison in Minnesota now has a 2.4 recidivism rate. Only 2.4 percent of the people that graduate go back to crime. You can be transformed. Christ does transform us. He gives us not only different desires, but He gives us the habits by which we live that way.

CHAPTER 8

America's Need for God*

by Jerry Newcombe

Unless the Lord build the house, they labor in vain who build it . . ."
Psalm 127:1

Our nation's Christian heritage is a precious gift from God. It is being squandered in our time, as the masses lift up the ungodly and perverted as praiseworthy.

If America gets completely cut off from our roots, how can we last—at least as a great nation? The psalmist asks, *"If the foundations are destroyed, what can the righteous do?"*[1] But whenever it seems bleakest, then God often intervenes.

Anyone who would deny that we are in a culture war does not seem to be very discerning to me. It is possible that America might not last. Nowhere is it decreed that our nation will last forever. Other nations have arisen and failed. We may just continue to implode and become a shell of what we once were.

We do well to learn from our rich history about the origins of this nation. In this chapter, we want to feature some considerations concerning the role of prayer at key points in our history.

In 1787, during the Constitutional Convention, the delegates hit an impasse. They had spent nearly two months trying to frame a new governing document and had barely made any progress. The whole exercise appeared fruitless and might even have come to a halt. At that time, the elderly statesman among them, Dr. Benjamin Franklin, reminded them they had forgotten to pray. We will learn more about his amazing speech momentarily.

Unfortunately, we often think of prayer as a last resort, just as our founding fathers did. "Pray—if all else fails." One could picture a figurine of praying hands enclosed in a glass frame on a wall (in place of a fire extinguisher) with a caption: "In case of emergency, break glass."

I truly believe that if America is to ever experience a rebirth, we are in great need of breaking that glass—and not just during emergencies. Actually, we are in great need of making prayer a dominant part of our lives.

Only with God's help can America be renewed. He is the One who can truly bring about change. Without His help, we cannot hope for what Abraham Lincoln called "a new birth of freedom."

National Days of Prayer During the Revolution

The founders of this nation certainly thought prayer was important. Do you know how many times Congress called for national days of prayer, humiliation, and fasting during the American War for Independence? Fifteen separate times. In addition, several of the colonies had their own colony-wide days of prayer. In fact, David Barton says, "Between 1633 and 1812, there were over 1,700 prayer proclamations issued in the colonies, where the governor would call the state to an annual day of prayer and fasting, annual day of prayer and of thanksgiving."

None of these were like some of today's political prayers, which could just as well be addressed, "To whom it may concern." For example, when John Hancock was the Governor of Massachusetts, he made an official Thanksgiving proclamation on October 5, 1791, in which he prayed for God's prosperity: "…that all may bow to the Scepter of our LORD JESUS CHRIST, and the whole Earth be filled with his Glory." [Emphasis his.] Hancock prayed that the day would come soon that Christ the King would reign on earth.

Revision of the Articles

The delegates to what we now know as the Constitutional Convention originally met to revise the Articles of Confederation (1777), our first governing document as a nation. During the early days of the Convention, they agreed that the Articles were not working; they gave too much power to the states and too little authority to the national government, which was anemic.

In Federalist Paper No. 30 Alexander Hamilton had written that the United States was at the precipice of collapse under the Articles. "In America … the government of the Union has gradually dwindled into a state of decay, approaching nearly to annihilation." The entire experiment in self-government might soon find its way onto "the ash heap of history" (to quote Ronald Reagan in a different context).

So here were all these men of Congress meeting initially to discuss how to revise the Articles, and then how to create a more workable document (which we now know as the United States Constitution). After a grueling May and June, they had made very little headway. The largest impasse dealt with representation of the big states versus the medium states versus the little states. (The ultimate solution was a House of Representatives that reflected the population of each state with a Senate that provided equal representation for each state, regardless of the size of its population. But that was to come later.)

The Atmosphere at the Convention

Men were coming and going at this convention held in Philadelphia, the same place they had framed and adopted the Declaration of

Independence. (We now call it Independence Hall.) Some were leaving because they had to get back to their business concerns—perhaps others because they felt their time was better spent elsewhere.

The days were hot and stifling. So were the nights. This was long before the days of air-conditioning and electric fans. Flies and mosquitoes were a problem.

Tempers flared. Some of the delegates liked to hear themselves speak, even if they had little to say in the conflict. (By some descriptions, Luther Martin, the delegate from Maryland who later refused to sign the Constitution, fits this category.) Through it all, George Washington sat silently, stoically, even if his patience was tried on occasion through the whole ordeal.

Finally, on June 28, the elderly Ben Franklin struggled to his feet and made one of the great speeches in American history. However, I find that it is virtually unknown among secular people. The average high school student knows nothing about Franklin's talk, which is missing from most books about American history or even the Constitution. (I never learned about it until I read Gary DeMar's book, *God and Government,* in 1984.) You could interview a hundred Americans, and probably less than 2 percent have heard of this speech. (Many of them would assume no such thing took place since they assume "the founding fathers intended a completely secular government.") You could attend the tours at Independence Hall and not learn anything about it. You could watch the talking heads on Sunday morning—the political pundits of our age—and not even be aware of its having taken place.

We can be thankful that Franklin's speech can be found in many of the books on America's Christian heritage. Furthermore, it can be found in the original material from the Convention. James Madison, delegate from Virginia, who is sometimes thought of as the "Father of the Constitution" or its chief architect, took detailed notes at the Convention.

Benjamin Franklin's Marvelous Speech

Ben Franklin was the oldest, and perhaps, most respected delegate at the Constitutional Convention—the only person who could possibly have been respected more was General Washington, the hero of the late war. Franklin's plea for prayer could be viewed essentially as a turning point at the Convention. Before his speech, the men were "spinning their wheels," so to speak. After the speech, they began to find traction and were able to accomplish something substantial.

Here's what Dr. Benjamin Franklin said on June 28, 1787 (reproduced, as in the original):

> Mr. President:
>
> The small progress we have made after 4 or 5 weeks close attendance & continual reasonings with each other—our different sentiments on almost every question, several of the last producing as many noes as ayes, is methinks a melancholy proof of the imperfection of the Human Understanding.
>
> We indeed seem to feel our own want of political wisdom, since we have been running about in search of it. We have gone back to ancient history for models of Government, and examined the different forms of those Republics which, having been formed with the seeds of their own dissolution, now no longer exist. And we have viewed Modern States all round Europe, but find none of their Constitutions suitable to our circumstances.
>
> In this situation of this Assembly, groping as it were in the dark to find political truth, and scarce able to distinguish it when presented to us, how has it happened, Sir, that we have not hitherto once thought of humbly applying to the Father of lights to illuminate our understanding?

In the beginning of the Contest with G. Britain, when we were sensible of danger, we had daily prayer in this room for Divine protection. Our prayers, Sir, were heard, & they were graciously answered. All of us who were engaged in the struggle must have observed frequent instances of a Superintending Providence in our favor.

To that kind Providence we owe this happy opportunity of consulting in peace on the means of establishing our future national felicity. And have we now forgotten that powerful Friend? or do we imagine we no longer need His assistance?

I have lived, Sir, a long time, and the longer I live, the more convincing proofs I see of this truth—that God Governs in the affairs of men. And if a sparrow cannot fall to the ground without His notice, is it probable that an empire can rise without His aid?

We have been assured, Sir, in the Sacred Writings, that "except the Lord build the House, they labor in vain that build it." I firmly believe this; and I also believe that without his concurring aid we shall succeed in this political building no better than the Builders of Babel: We shall be divided by our partial local interests; our projects will be confounded, and we ourselves shall become a reproach and bye word down to future ages.

And what is worse, mankind may hereafter from this unfortunate instance, despair of establishing Governments by Human wisdom and leave it to chance, war and conquest.

I therefore beg leave to move—that henceforth prayers imploring the assistance of Heaven, and its blessing on our deliberations, be held in this Assembly every morning before we proceed to business, and that one or more of the clergy of this city be requested to officiate in that service.[2]

Here one of the least religious of the founding fathers, a man whose beliefs were not orthodox, was asking the delegates to remember God and seek His help.

New Jersey delegate Jonathan Dayton described the impression the old man made on the rest of them:

> The Doctor sat down; and never did I behold a countenance at once so dignified and delighted as was that of Washington at the close of the address; nor were the members of the convention generally less affected. The words of the venerable Franklin fell upon our ears with a weight and authority, even greater than we may suppose an oracle to have had in a Roman senate![3]

That's quite an impression.

Immediately Roger Sherman of Connecticut (one of the few of the founding fathers to sign both the Declaration and the Constitution) seconded the motion. Then the delegates bandied Franklin's suggestion back and forth. They did not officially accept the motion because their treasury was empty—there was no money to hire a chaplain. Franklin noted with dismay that it was not accepted, as he thought. However, they did not officially vote down his suggestion.

Instead, they agreed on an alternative that accepted the spirit and gist of Franklin's proposal. The alternative was provided by Edmund Jennings Randolph of Virginia, who suggested that:

1. a sermon be preached—at the official request of the Convention—the next week on the Fourth of July to

mark the anniversary of Independence, and

2.   prayers be said in the Convention every morning.

What impact did Dr. Franklin's request have on the progress of the Constitutional Convention? New Jersey Delegate Jonathan Dayton tells us what it was like on July 2, just a few days later, when they reconvened for the first time since Franklin's speech: "We assembled again; and . . . every unfriendly feeling had been expelled, and a spirit of conciliation had been cultivated."[4]

Then on the Fourth of July, the entire Convention attended a special service in the Reformed Calvinistic Lutheran Church, where they heard a sermon by Rev. William Rogers, wherein he prayed:

> We fervently recommend to the fatherly notice . . .
> our federal convention . . . Favor them, from day to
> day, with thy inspiring presence; be their wisdom and
> strength; enable them to devise such measures as may
> prove happy instruments in healing all divisions and
> prove the good of the great whole; . . . that the United
> States of America may form one example of a free and
> virtuous government. . . . May we . . . continue, under
> the influence of republican virtue, to partake of all the
> blessings of cultivated and Christian society.[5]

Think of how "unconstitutional" all this may appear to modern ears. Here all the government officials are attending a *Christian* service in a *Christian* church, where they are being encouraged to act as wise *Christians* as they choose how the nation's *Christian* subjects should be governed.

Don't these men know the U.S. Constitution? What about "the separation of church and state"? Oh, wait—these are the men who *gave* us the Constitution, and all of this took place as they were writing the document. Looking at Franklin's speech shows us how far we have strayed from our history, our purpose, our mission.

I remember engaging in a series of correspondence by email with an acquaintance who was of the persuasion that the founding fathers were basically secular humanists. When I sent him the details of Ben Franklin's appeal to prayer, he ceased further communication. The facts of history speak for themselves.

Another Prayer in Another American Legislature

We have gained a small glimpse of the founding fathers' deep abiding respect for prayer and its role in building up the American "empire" for good purposes. To this day throughout America, our Congress, our Senate, and also the state legislatures open in prayer. During the 1990s, a pastor was invited to say the opening prayer at the statehouse in Kansas. He chose to be anything, but politically correct. Paul Harvey, the noted radio commentator, described the event in this way:

"DOES GOD EVER KNOW!"

Man, oh, man [does God ever know]! They won't invite Pastor Joe to the Kansas State Legislature again.

They invited Pastor Joe Wright of Wichita's Central Christian Church to deliver the invocation—and he told God on them!

Now, God knows what they've been up to! No sooner had their guest chaplain concluded his prayer than three Democrats on the state legislature were on their feet at microphones protesting, "He can't talk like that about us!" Rep. Delbert Gross considered the invocation gross, calling it "divisive," "sanctimonious," and "overbearing."

Rep. David Haley called it "blasphemous and ignorant."

Rep. Sabrina Standifer echoed the indignation.

What in the world did Pastor Joe say in Topeka that

incited the righteous wrath of three Democrats from Hays and Kansas City?

I've secured the entire text of the invocation, so you can evaluate it for yourself and decide.

"Heavenly Father, we come before you today to ask Your forgiveness and to seek Your direction and guidance.

We know Your Word says, 'Woe to those who call evil good,' but that is exactly what we have done. We have lost our spiritual equilibrium and inverted our values.

We confess that we have ridiculed the absolute truth of Your Word in the name of moral pluralism.

We have worshipped other gods and called it "multi-culturalism."

We have endorsed perversion and called it an "alternative lifestyle."

We have exploited the poor and called it "a lottery."

We have neglected the needy and called it "self-preservation."

We have rewarded laziness and called it "welfare."

In the name of "choice," we have killed our unborn.

In the name of "right to life," we have killed abortionists.

We have neglected to discipline our children and called it "building esteem."

We have abused power and called it "political savvy."

We've coveted our neighbors' possessions and called it "taxes."

We've polluted the air with profanity and pornography and called it "freedom of expression."

We've ridiculed the time-honored values of our forefathers and called it "enlightenment."

Search us, O God, and know our hearts today. Try us, and show us [if there be] any wicked in us. Cleanse us from every sin, and set us free.

Guide and bless these men and women who have been sent here by the people of Kansas and who have been ordained by You to govern this great state.

Grant them Your wisdom to rule, and may their decisions direct us to the center of Your will.

I ask it in the name of your Son, the living Savior, Jesus Christ. Amen."[6]

No wonder this gentleman will not be invited back to say an invocation. But his spiritual indictment on contemporary America is an excellent one. This reminds me of what Dr. D. James Kennedy once said:

> My friends, the hour is late. I think it is important that each one of us carefully consider the Biblical teachings about man, society, the state, and the purpose of life while we still have the freedom to consider them at all.
>
> God has placed us in this free land, yet bit by bit, piece by piece, we have been selling our birthright for a mess of pottage. We have been fearful to stand up and exercise the talents and the abilities God has given us. We have been unwilling to trust Him to provide for our needs, and so we have sold our birthright of freedom for the security of the state, not realizing that we are selling ourselves into bondage.[7]

If My People

Did you hear about the open prayer sessions in a public high school? Probably not. Several students and even teachers huddled together in a room at this school. Someone asked if there was anyone religious in the room that might be able to lead them in prayer. One of the students volunteered, and they held prayer there at school during normal school hours. What happened next? An ACLU lawsuit.

Not exactly. These students and teachers were fleeing the bloodshed at Columbine High School on April 20, 1999 in Littleton, Colorado, the day of the massacre of twelve students and one teacher, and the double-suicides of the two murderers. Prayer came to the public school in America on that day—only it came too late.

Ours is a nation in need of prayer, in need of a spiritual revival. If America is truly to be renewed, it will not be through the political process, as important as that is. I believe we need a renewed vision, for *"where there is no vision, the people perish."*[8] God can do the impossible, and so, indeed, we can experience a renewal in this land. If there is to be a new birth of freedom in America, then what we need most of all is a genuine revival.

The most appropriate of all Bible verses that spells out the remedy for a nation that has lost its way is 2 Chronicles 7:14: *"[I]f My people who are called by My name will humble themselves and pray and seek My face, and turn from their wicked ways, then I will hear from heaven, and will forgive their sin and heal their land."* (NKJV)

America began in part because of the spiritual movement in the mid-18th century known as the Great Awakening. There was a special move of God's Spirit as He used men of God, in particular, Jonathan Edwards and George Whitefield, to preach the gospel and convert many. The impact on society was profound. John Adams said that revolution of 1776 was essentially the political outworking of the *spiritual* revolution that had occurred the generation before; i.e., the Great Awakening.

The great British historian, Paul Johnson, author of *A History of the American People,* noted:

> As we have seen, America had been founded primar-
> ily for religious purposes, and the Great Awakening

had been the original dynamic of the continental movement for independence. The Americans were overwhelmingly church-going, much more so than the English, whose rule they rejected.[9]

George Whitefield was the greatest evangelist of the First Great Awakening. When he first came to Boston in 1740, he saw the outward veneer of religiosity, which was often missing the inner reality. Here is what he wrote on October 12, 1740:

> Boston is a large populous place, and very wealthy. It has the form of religion kept up, but has lost much of its power. I have not heard of any remarkable stir for years. Ministers and people are obliged to confess that the love of many is waxed cold. Both seem too conformed to the world . . .

This was a great example of Cotton Mather's axiom, "Religion brought forth Prosperity, and the daughter destroyed the mother."[10]

Boston prospered because Boston was religious. By 1740, too much of that religion was an outward show. But Whitefield and company helped to change that, by the grace of God, in the First Great Awakening.

Dr. D. James Kennedy, used to say that the only thing that can really change America for the better is true revival. The first Great Awakening, of course, helped lead to the founding of America. The Second Great Awakening helped lead to the end of the evil of slavery. Now, we need a Third Great Awakening. Such a move of God is what this nation desperately needs.

Conclusion

The great news is that pastors and laypeople can play an active role in saving our nation's Christian heritage. We have freedom now.

But it may be lost one day because of our apathy, not overnight, but over time. May that never be!

Our second president, John Adams, once gave a solemn warning to us:

> Posterity! You will never know how much it cost the present generation to preserve your freedom! I hope you will make good use of it! If you do not, I shall repent it in Heaven that I ever took half the pains to preserve it![11]

Our 26th president, Theodore Roosevelt, said, "Fear God; and take your own part!"[12]

We may not succeed, but what kind of an America do we want to leave for our children and grandchildren?

Finally, consider the words of our sixth president, John Quincy Adams, son of our second president, John Adams. With his profound axiom, we close: "Duty is ours; results are God's."[13]

---

* From *The Book That Made America: How the Bible Helped Form Our Nation*[14]

CHAPTER 9

A New Era of Cultural Engagement

by Frank Wright

Righteousness exalts a nation, but sin is a reproach to any people.
PROVERBS 14:34

In 1949 Emilio Franco regained his speaking voice. Mr. Franco was a West Virginia coal miner who had been rendered mute by a nervous system disorder. In the summer of that year, Mr. Franco and his family vacationed in New York, and they made their way to Coney Island.

While there, he rode the terrifying Cyclone roller coaster. And it was on one of the Cyclone's steep descents that Mr. Franco began screaming. Later, while disembarking, Emilio Franco spoke his first words since World War II: He said: . . . "I feel sick."

These many years later we can hardly open the morning newspaper, or watch the evening news, or check our favorite new website without having a "Maalox Moment" of our own.

We live, it seems, in an age of great moral and spiritual deficits, with the relativistic thinking of our time producing a culture that seems to be on moral life-support. And by any objective diagnosis the patient (that is, the culture) is not doing well. The individual, the family, the church, the civil government—even a decent and civil society—today all are under assault.

A Clash of Orthodoxies

All of this is so because we live today in a culture engaged in what Princeton professor Robert George calls a "clash of orthodoxies." In our day, transcendent truth faces withering fire from secularists whose only "orthodoxy" is doing what seems right in their own eyes.

Yet, this clash, which dates to the dawn of human history, has taken an ominous turn in recent years, with the voices of atheistic secularism attempting to marginalize and demonize their opponents by declaiming historic Christian teaching as "hate speech." All of which is part of a concerted effort to drive every vestige of religious expression from the public square.

At the same time, Biblical worldview education is at a low ebb, with research indicating less than ten percent of self-identified Christians possess a truly Biblical worldview. Perhaps even more portentous is the research showing only six percent of Christian churches have a pastor teaching a Biblical world and life view.

As a result, few Christians are able to articulate the first principle of a Biblical worldview: the sovereignty of God over His creation. Yet, the implications of God's sovereignty are profound.

At a minimum, God's sovereignty over His creation means God is sovereign over business and law and education and medicine and community service, and all of the institutions of culture—including (and maybe especially) government and politics.

God's sovereign rule over His creation also has significant implications for each of us on a deeply personal level. As children of the Living God by faith in Jesus Christ, our faith is not something relegated only to the realm of personal morality and ethics. Our calling is to live out our faith in the wider world for the good of others and for the glory of God. In doing so, we have the clear commands of God to engage the world around us.

Cultural Engagement

First, we are commanded to bring the Gospel of Jesus Christ to the world. Theologians refer to this as the "Great Commission" of Christ, because it offers to mankind the only true hope for this life and the life to come. In its fulfillment, we are preaching the Gospel, making disciples, and bearing witness to the reality of Christ in our lives and to His offer of freedom from the guilt and punishment of sin that comes with faith in Him.

Second, we also are commanded to bring the mind of Christ to the world around us—what theologians call the "Cultural Mandate." In it we bring the Word of God to bear on the institutions of the broader culture, along with the great moral, ethical, and cultural questions of our day.

These two commands comprise the ethic of Christian cultural engagement. And it was this engagement that overcame the Dark Ages. It was Christians applying the mind of Christ—applying the Word of God—to the world around them that shaped western civilization as we know it.

And it was the Protestant Reformation that put the Word of God into the hands of common people, which quite naturally led to the birth of widely available education—as people thirsted to read so that they could apprehend the Word of God for themselves.

And that gave birth to freedoms never before realized on the face of the Earth, with the chief among those freedoms being freedom of religion.

My mentor and friend, Dr. D. James Kennedy, once said: "Religious freedom was unknown in the world until it was established in America."

Did you know that?

There was some religious toleration, but true religious freedom existed nowhere on Earth before the founding of America. This is one of the reasons why we refer to our nation as the American Experiment.

As former Yale professor William Lyon Phelps observed: "Our civilization is founded on the Bible. More of our ideas, our wisdom, our philosophy, our literature, our art, our ideals come from the Bible than from all other books combined."[1]

Even *Newsweek* magazine, hardly a bastion of conservative Christian ideals, made this observation on December 27, 1982: "For centuries, the Bible has exerted an unrivaled influence on American culture, politics, and social life. Now historians are discovering that the Bible, perhaps even more than the Constitution, is our founding document."

But as we look around us today, we cannot help but say: "My, how the mighty have fallen."

Instead we live today in a world seemingly running headlong away from any notion of Biblical morality. We live in a time when the rabidly mendacious can call historic Christianity "hate speech" and a credulous (or perhaps complicit) mainstream media nods approvingly.

So, we find ourselves in this great clash of orthodoxies at a time when the church seems ill equipped to stand and defend truth. And nowhere are the implications of these deficits more evident than in the arena of leadership training—especially in the public policy arena.

Now, at this point, we could wring our hands and bemoan the cultural tide. But if we look at the world around us with eyes of faith, we should see that we live in a defining time for people of faith. We live in a day of opportunity.

The Center for Christian Leadership

Here is a question for you: What would our political landscape look like if we had leaders with an unshakable Christian conviction, a well-grounded Biblical worldview, and a mastery of the principles, purposes, and political philosophy of the United States Constitution?

What if those leaders had carefully studied the application of that political philosophy to the great moral, ethical, economic, and cultural questions of the day? And what if those leaders were well schooled in the critically important skills of communication, debate, negotiation, and planning? And what if all that education, training, and equipping took place before those leaders were elevated to high office?

What would you have?

Some would say you have 1776. You would have leaders birthed and reared as the Founding Generation—a generation that produced statesmen who literally changed the face of the world.

And where are such leaders today? Well, we do have some; but far too few.

Friends, if we carefully consider the Founding Generation, one differential attribute stands out among all others. Unsurprisingly that quality is lacking in our day—indeed it has been missing in action for generations.

What is that attribute? In a word—preparation.

In the past, many Christians have responded to the Biblical imperative of cultural engagement. Yet, increasingly, the public square has surrendered to the forces of secularism, with the influence of a Biblical worldview in the public policy arena dramatically diminished.

Often those answering a calling to public service for Christ have entered that very challenging environment without being properly prepared and equipped to do so. Still, these men and women deserve praise, for they at least have stood for battle. But we have not stood with them in full—at least in terms of the resources and efforts needed to prepare them for effective service.

The D. James Kennedy Center for Christian Leadership represents a new era of leadership training—at least for those who name Jesus Christ as Savior and Lord. The Center was birthed to address this deficit of preparation for Biblical cultural engagement—especially for leadership service in government and the public policy arena.

The Center for Christian Leadership is a comprehensive and intensive leadership training program, based in Washington, D.C.

It will provide face-to-face instruction by a distinguished faculty of experts; the training focuses on developing the necessary *Skill Set*, expanding the necessary *Knowledge Base*, and studying their *Strategic Application*.

The *Skill Set* training seeks to expand competency in communications, debate, media messaging, negotiation, and planning. The *Knowledge Base* training seeks to expand understanding and application of a Biblical worldview and political philosophy, within a robust Constitutional framework. And the *Strategic Application* training focuses on communications strategy, political strategy, and the strategy of marketplace messaging.

The faculty expert specialties include: theology, constitutional law, education, communications, media, organizational development, and political strategy.

A Call to Action

John Wesley said: "Give me 100 men that hate nothing but sin, and love Jesus Christ, and we will shake England for God,"—and they did.

That spirit captures the essence of the Center for Christian Leadership.

In contrast to the much-needed emphasis on grass roots political mobilization, the Center seeks to uniquely prepare select leaders who by God's grace will seek to attain significant positions of influence and authority in government and the public policy arena.

The specific goal of the Center is straightforward: Train 300 leaders per year for each of the next 10 years.

From where will these future leaders come? How will we identify those who are ready and willing and able? What qualifications are necessary to be invited to participate in the Center for Christian Leadership—for, yes, this is an invitation-only training program.

We begin, of course, with prayer, for above all things, we are looking for men and women with a heart after God's own heart.

We are looking for those with both humility and determination. We are looking for a gifted and teachable cohort. We are looking for those willing to invest their time, significant resources, and efforts to pursue a unique calling.

Now, some will say: "Leadership training. Really?" "But the need is so great. The time is now."

That is essentially what a young seminary student once said to Dr. Billy Graham. "Am I wasting my time here in seminary, when the need for Gospel ministry is so great?" Dr. Graham sagely replied: "Young man, the time a woodsman spends sharpening his axe is not wasted."

A Personal and Practical Faith

At the beginning of the last century, one of the towering intellectual figures in British public life was Gilbert Keith Chesterton: G.K. Chesterton as we know him today.

He was a journalist, a writer, a social critic, and a theologian. His many books are still widely available today.

Chesterton was the kind of intellectual powerhouse who had an opinion on everything.

As such, his comments, on a wide range of subjects, were often solicited by his literary friends. On one occasion he was asked: "What book would you like if you were to be cast adrift on a lonely Pacific island and were permitted to have only one book?"

One friend, knowing him to be a religious man, said: "I suppose you would choose the Bible. Chesterton's eyes twinkled, and he said: "No, not this time."

Another friend, knowing of his broad literary interest, said: "I'd wager you would take a copy of Shakespeare." "You would lose that wager," Chesterton replied.

"Well, what would you choose?" they asked.

Chesterton smiled broadly and said: "If I were stranded on a lonely island in the Pacific, the one book I would choose, of all the books in the world, would be one titled: "A Manual on How to Build a Ship."

Chesterton was an intensely practical man; yet he was also a devout Christian.

Both of these qualities are needed to stand for truth in a culture being nursed on lies. The need is great, and the hour does seem late, from a human perspective. Yet, God often has chosen to glorify Himself by doing great things through small numbers of strategically placed people. We see this throughout the Old and New Testament Scriptures.

The end and aim of the D. James Kennedy Center for Christian Leadership is to equip a highly select group of leaders who recognize the need for Biblical truth in government and are striving for the highest position of influence they can attain in the arena of government and public policy.

These are men and women who recognize Christ's sovereignty over all His creation—including government and politics. These are people whose calling supersedes career; people whose vocation is first and foremost a kingdom endeavor.

When their training is complete, these individuals, relying upon the grace of God, will grow where they are planted, seizing every opportunity to bring the mind of Christ to bear in their lives, their work, and their relationships.

They commit to being lifelong learners, continuing to build on the foundation established in their lives. They commit to prayerfully, patiently, and strategically seek opportunities to rise in levels of leadership, wisdom, and influence. They commit to doing all these things for the glory of God.

Let Freedom Ring

If true freedom will continue to ring across our land, if this nation will continue to be a "shining city on a hill" and a beacon of light and hope to the world, then a new generation of leaders must rise up and stand for truth.

We ask those with vision, a love for Christ, and a love for this great nation to join us in this kingdom endeavor.

America will not be transformed by the next set of laws or the next business innovation, but by the next generation of leaders. Leaders who are fully equipped and determined to stand for truth as God gives them opportunity to serve.

Perhaps you will be one of them.

National Proclamations of Prayer

by William J. Federer

1620's, Edward Winslow, administrator of the Plymouth Colony, recounted the Pilgrims' experiences:

"Drought and the like considerations moved not only every good man privately to enter into examination with his own estate between God and his conscience, and so to humiliation before Him, but also to humble ourselves together before the Lord by fasting and prayer"[3]

1668, the Commonwealth of Virginia enacted:

"The 27th of August appointed for a day of humiliation, fasting, and prayer, to implore God's mercy."[4]

May 24, 1773, the Virginia House of Burgesses approved a Day of Fasting, Humiliation and Prayer:

"This House, being deeply impressed with apprehension of the great dangers to be derived to British America from the hostile invasion of the city of Boston in our Sister Colony of Massachusetts Bay,

"whose commerce and harbor are, on the first day of June next, to be stopped by an armed force, deem it highly necessary that the said first day of June be set apart, by the members of this House, as a Day of Fasting, Humiliation and Prayer,

"devoutly to implore the Divine interposition, for averting the heavy calamity which threatens destruction to our civil rights and the evils of civil war; to give us one heart and mind firmly opposed, by all just and proper means, every injury to American rights;

"and that the minds of His Majesty and his Parliament, may be inspired from above with wisdom, moderation and justice, to remove from the loyal people of America all cause of danger from a continued pursuit of measures pregnant with their ruin."[5]

April 19, 1775, Governor Jonathan Trumbull declared a Day of Fasting and Prayer for the Connecticut Colony, that:

"God would graciously pour out His Holy Spirit on us to bring us to a thorough Repentance and effectual Reformation that our iniquities may not be our ruin;

"that He would restore, preserve and secure the Liberties of this and all the other British American colonies, and make the Land a mountain of Holiness, and Habitation of Righteousness forever."[6]

June 12, 1775, the Continental Congress declared a Day of Public Humiliation, Fasting, and Prayer:

"As the Great Governor of the World, by his supreme and universal Providence, not only conducts the course of nature with unerring wisdom and rectitude, but frequently influences the minds of men to serve the wise and gracious purposes of His indispensable duty . . .

"This Congress, therefore, considering the present critical, alarming and calamitous state of these Colonies, do earnestly recommend . . . that we may with united hearts and voices, unfeignedly confess and deplore our many sins and offer up our joint supplications to the All-wise, Omnipotent and merciful Disposer of all Events, humbly beseeching Him to forgive our iniquities, to remove our present calamities. . . . that virtue and true religion may revive and flourish throughout our land

"and that America may soon behold a gracious interposition of Heaven for the redress of her many grievances, the restoration of her invaded Rights, a reconciliation with the parent State, on terms constitutional and honorable to both - and that her civil and religious Privileges may be secured to the latest posterity.

"And it is recommended to Christians of all denominations to assemble for public worship and to abstain from servile Labour and Recreations of said day. By order of the Congress, John Hancock, President."[7]

March 16, 1776, the Continental Congress passed without dissent a National Day of Humiliation, Fasting and Prayer:

"The Congress . . . desirous . . . to have people of all ranks and degrees duly impressed with a solemn sense of God's superintending Providence, and of their duty, devoutly to rely . . . on his aid and direction . . .

"We do earnestly recommend Friday, the 17th day of May be observed by the colonies as a day of humiliation, fasting, and prayer; that we may, with united hearts, confess and bewail our manifold sins and transgressions, and, by sincere repentance and amendment of life, appease God's righteous displeasure, and, through the merits and mediation of Jesus Christ, obtain this pardon and forgiveness."[8]

May 15, 1776, General George Washington issued the order:

"The Continental Congress having ordered Friday the 17th instant to be observed as a day of fasting, humiliation, and prayer, humbly to supplicate the mercy of Almighty God, that it would please Him to pardon all our manifold sins and transgressions, and to prosper the arms of the United Colonies, and finally establish the peace and freedom of America upon a solid and lasting foundation;

"the General commands all officers and soldiers to pay strict obedience to the orders of the Continental Congress; that, by their unfeigned and pious observance of their religious duties, they may incline the Lord and Giver of victory to prosper our arms.[9]

On March 30, 1863, President Abraham Lincoln issued a Proclamation appointing a National Day of Humiliation, Fasting and Prayer:

"Whereas, the Senate of the United States devoutly recognizing the Supreme Authority and just Government of Almighty God in all the affairs of men and of nations, has, by a resolution, requested the President to designate and set apart a day for national prayer and humiliation; and

"Whereas, it is the duty of nations as well as of men to own their dependence upon the overruling power of God, to confess their sins and transgressions in humble sorrow yet with assured hope that genuine repentance will lead to mercy and pardon, and to recognize the sublime truth, announced in the Holy Scriptures and proven by all history: that those nations only are blessed whose God is the Lord;

"And, insomuch as we know that, by His divine law, nations like individuals are subjected to punishments and chastisement in this world, may we not justly fear that the awful calamity of civil war, which now desolates the land may be but a punishment inflicted upon us for our presumptuous sins to the needful end of our national reformation as a whole people? "We have been the recipients of the choicest bounties of Heaven. We have been preserved these many years in peace and prosperity. We have grown in numbers, wealth and power as no other nation has ever grown.

"But we have forgotten God. We have forgotten the gracious Hand which preserved us in peace, and multiplied and enriched and strengthened us; and we have vainly imagined, in the deceitfulness of our hearts, that all these blessings were produced by some superior wisdom and virtue of our own.

"Intoxicated with unbroken success, we have become too self-sufficient to feel the necessity of redeeming and preserving grace, too proud to pray to the God that made us! It behooves us then to humble ourselves before the offended Power, to confess our national sins and to pray for clemency and forgiveness.

"Now, therefore, in compliance with the request and fully concurring in the view of the Senate, I do, by this my proclamation, designate and set apart Thursday, the 30th day of April, 1863, as a day of national humiliation, fasting and prayer.

"And I do hereby request all the people to abstain on that day from their ordinary secular pursuits, and to unite, at their several places of public worship and their respective homes, in keeping the day holy to the Lord and devoted to the humble discharge of the religious duties proper to that solemn occasion.

"All this being done, in sincerity and truth, let us then rest humbly in the hope authorized by the Divine teachings, that the united cry of the nation will be heard on high and answered with blessing no less than the pardon of our national sins and the restoration of our now divided and suffering country to its former happy condition of unity and peace."[10]

June 17, 1952, President Harry S. Truman issued Proclamation 2978, declaring an annual National Day of Prayer:

"Whereas from the earliest days of our history our people have been accustomed to turn to Almighty God for help and guidance; and Whereas in times of national crisis when we are striving to strengthen the foundations of peace and security we stand in special need of divine support; and

"Whereas the Congress, by a joint resolution approved on April 17, 1952 (66 Stat. 64), has provided that the President 'shall set aside and proclaim a suitable day each year, other than Sunday, as a National Day of Prayer, on which the people of the United States may turn to God in prayer and meditation'; and

"Whereas I deem it fitting that this Day of Prayer coincide with the anniversary of the adoption of the Declaration of Independence, which published to the world this Nation's 'firm reliance on the protection of Divine Providence':

"Now, Therefore, I, Harry S. Truman, President of the United States of America, do hereby proclaim Friday, July 4, 1952, as a National Day of Prayer, on which all of us, in our churches, in our homes, and in our hearts, may beseech God to grant us wisdom to know the course which we should follow, and strength and patience to pursue that course steadfastly.

"May we also give thanks to Him for His constant watchfulness over us in every hour of national prosperity and national peril. In Witness Thereof, I have hereunto set my hand and caused the Seal of the United States of America to be affixed. Done at the City of Washington this 17th day of June in the year of our Lord nineteen hundred and fifty-two, and of the Independence of the United States of America the one hundred and seventy-sixth. Harry S. Truman."[1]

January 25, 1988, President Ronald Reagan signed Public Law 100-307 declaring the National Day of Prayer to be held on the first Thursday of each May:

"Be it enacted by the Senate and House of Representatives of the United States of America in Congress assembled, That the joint resolution entitled 'Joint Resolution to provide for setting aside an appropriate day as a National Day of Prayer,' approved April 17, 1952 (Public Law 82-324; 66 Stat. 64), is amended by striking 'a suitable day each year, other than a Sunday', and inserting in lieu thereof 'the first Thursday in May in each year.'"[2]

ENDNOTES

Chapter 1 — Is There Any Hope for America?

1   http://www.pewresearch.org/fact-tank/2017/09/14/as-u-s-marriage-rate-hovers-at-50-education-gap-in-marital-status-widens/

2   http://www.pewforum.org/2012/10/09/nones-on-the-rise/

3   https://www.guttmacher.org/fact-sheet/induced-abortion-united-states

4   Francis Schaeffer, "A Christian Manifesto," Coral Ridge Presbyterian Church, Ft. Lauderdale, 1982.

5   Sen. James Lankford, taken from an interview conducted by the D. James Kennedy Center for Christian Statesmanship, broadcast nationwide 2016, www.statesman.org.

6   Romans 1:18-32.

7   http://cityobservatory.org/wp-content/files/CityObservatory_Less_In_Common.pdf

8   http://www.myhopewithbillygraham.org.uk/not_a_statistic/

9   Tom Clegg & Warren Bird, *Lost in America* (Loveland, CO: Group Publishing, 2001), 25.

10   Matthew 4:19.

11   Mark 16:15, NKJV.

12   https://www.census.gov/popclock/

13   Thom Rainer, *Surprising Insights from the Unchurched and Proven Ways to Reach Them* (Grand Rapids, MI: Zondervan, 2001).

14   William J. Bennett, "Does Honor Have a Future?" The Forrestal Lecture delivered before the United States Naval Academy, November 24, 1997.

15   Bob Sjogren, *Unveiled at Last*, YWAM Publishing, 1992.

16   Bill Bright & John N. Damoose, *Red Sky in the Morning* (Orlando, FL: New Life Publications, 1998), 153.

17   Clegg & Bird, *Lost in America*, 16.

18   Taken from a 1988 Gallup Poll published at: http://www.gallup.com/poll/11770/eternal-destinations-americans-believe-heaven-hell.aspx.

19   Admiral William Frederick Jr. was an American Naval Officer during World War II, 1882 to 1959.

20   http://www.christianitytoday.com/news/2013/july/missionaries-countries-sent-received-csgc-gordon-conwell.html

Chapter 2 — Freedom's Holy Light

1   John Adams wrote to his wife Abigail from Philadelphia on September, 16, 1774, of the debate over prayer:

> Having a leisure moment, while the Congress is assembling, I gladly embrace it to write you a line. When the Congress first met, Mr. Cushing made a motion that it should be opened with prayer. It was opposed by Mr. Jay, of New York, and Mr. Rutledge of South Carolina, because we were so divided in religious sentiments, some Episcopalians, some Quakers, some Anabaptists, some Presbyterians, and some Congregationalists, that we could not join in the same act of worship. Mr. Samuel Adams arose and said he was no bigot, and could hear a prayer from a gentleman of piety and virtue, who was at the same time a friend to his country. He was a stranger in Philadelphia, but had heard that Mr. Duché (Dushay they pronounce it) deserved that character, and therefore he moved that Mr. Duché, an Episcopal clergyman, might be desired to read prayers to the Congress, tomorrow morning. The motion was seconded and passed in the affirmative. Mr. Randolph, our president, waited on Mr. Duché, and received for an answer that if his health would permit he certainly would. Accordingly, next morning he appeared with his clerk and in his pontificals, and read several prayers in the established form; and then read the Collect for the seventh day of September, which was the thirty-fifth Psalm. You must remember this was the next morning after we heard the horrible rumor of the cannonade of Boston. I never saw a greater effect upon an audience. **It seemed as if Heaven had ordained that Psalm to be read on that morning**.
>
> After this Mr. Duché, unexpected to everybody, struck out into an extemporary prayer, which filled the bosom of every man present. I must confess I never heard a better prayer, or one so well pronounced. Episcopalian as he is, Dr. Cooper himself (Dr. Samuel Cooper, well known as a zealous patriot and pastor of the church in Brattle Square, Boston) never prayed with such fervor, such earnestness and pathos, and in language so elegant and sublime—for America, for the Congress, for the Province of Massachusetts Bay, and especially the town of Boston. It has had an excellent effect upon everybody here. I must beg you to read that Psalm. If there was any faith in the Sortes Biblicae, it would be thought providential. . . .

2   Cited in *One Nation Under God: An Anthology for Americans*, ed. Robert Gordon Smith (New York: Funk & Wagnalls, 1961), 39-40. Editor's Note: **The emphasis in all these quotes in this chapter have been added** by Dr. Lillback, to underscore the theme of Divine Providence.

3   *First Prayer in Congress—Beautiful Reminiscence* (Washington, D. C.: Library of Congress); John S. C. Abbot, *George Washington* (NY: Dodd, Mead & Co., 1875,

1917), 187.

4   Patrick Henry, "Give me liberty or give me death," March 23, 1775, in *The Annals of America* (Chicago et al.: Encyclopaedia Britannica, 1976), 2:323.

5   Continental Congress, Proclamation for a day of humiliation, fasting, and prayer, March 16, 1776. Library of Congress website: www.cdn.loc.gov

6   Our founders, early on, had a deep concern that religious bigotry would gain no foothold in the American government. Consider here Washington's classic words written on August 17, 1790 to the Hebrew Congregation in New Port, Rhode Island:

> Gentlemen: While I receive with much satisfaction your address replete with expressions of affection and esteem, I rejoice in the opportunity of assuring you that I shall always retain a grateful remembrance of the cordial welcome I experienced in my visit to New Port from all classes of Citizens. . . .The Citizens of the United States of America have a right to applaud themselves for having given to Mankind examples of an enlarged and liberal policy, a policy worthy of imitation. All possess alike liberty of conscience and immunities of citizenship. It is now no more that toleration is spoken of, as if it was by the indulgence of one class of people, that another enjoyed the exercise of their inherent natural rights. For happily the Government of the United Sates, which gives to bigotry no sanction, to persecution no assistance, requires only that they who live under its protection should demean themselves as good citizens, in giving it on all occasions their effectual support. . . .May the children of the Stock of Abraham, who dwell in this land, continue to merit and enjoy the good will of the other inhabitants, while every one shall sit in safety under his own vine and fig tree, and there shall be none to make him afraid. May the Father of all mercies scatter light and not darkness in our paths, and make us all in our several vocations useful here, and in his own due time and way everlastingly happy. G. Washington.

An example of the Christianity of our Founding Fathers in one of their Thanksgiving Proclamations can be found in the following dated November 1, 1777:

> Forasmuch as it is the indispensable duty of all men to adore the superintending providence of Almighty God; . . .they may join the penitent confession of their manifold sins, whereby they had forfeited every favour, and their humble and earnest supplication that it may please God, through the merits of Jesus Christ, mercifully to forgive and blot them out of remembrance; that it may please him graciously to afford his blessing on the governments of these states respectively. . . and to prosper the means of religion for the promotion and enlargement of that kingdom which consisteth "in righteousness, peace and joy in the Holy Ghost.

Many other examples of the faith of our founding fathers can be found in our nation's early congressional records. For example, see *The Journals of Congress*, March 1782, 138.

7   Benjamin Franklin, Treaty of Paris, September 3, 1783, in W. Cleon Skousen, *The Making of America* (Washington: The National Center for Constitutional Studies, 1985), 139.

8   The story of Washington meeting the Indians which he had battled in the wilderness many years earlier when General Braddock was killed can be found in *Recollections of Washington* by G.W. Parke Custis Washington, pp. 300-06. The account begins:

> The council fire was kindled, when the grand sachem addressed our Washington to the following effect:

> > "I am a chief and ruler over my tribes. My influence extends to the waters of the great lakes and to the far blue mountains. I have traveled a long and weary path that I might see the young warrior of the great battle. It was on the day when the white man's blood mixed with the streams of our forests that I first beheld this chief: I called to my young men and said, mark yon tall and daring warrior? He is not of the red-coat tribe--he hath an Indian's wisdom, and his warriors fight as we do—himself alone exposed. Quick, let your aim be certain, and he dies. Our rifles were leveled, rifles which, but for you, knew not how to miss-'twas all in vain, a power mightier far than we, shielded him from harm. He can not die in battle. I am old and soon shall be gathered to the great council fire of my fathers in the land of shades, but ere I go, there is something bids me speak in the voice of prophecy: Listen! *The Great Spirit protects that man, and guides his destinies—he will become the chief of nations, and a people yet unborn will hail him as the founder of a mighty empire!*

This story was also published as a play: *The Indian Prophecy, A National Drama*, in two Acts. Founded upon a most interesting and romantic occurrence in the life of General Washington. Performed at the Theatres of Philadelphia, Baltimore, and Washington. To which is prefixed, A Memoir of the Indian Prophecy, From *The Recollections and Private Memoirs of the Life and Character of Washington*. By The author of the *Recollections*. G. W. Parke Custis Washington, Georgetown, D.C. Published by James Thomas, 1828.

9   George Washington, August 17, 1790, an address to the Hebrew Congregation in Newport, Rhode Island. John Eidsmoe, *Christianity and the Constitution: The Faith of Our Founding Fathers* (Grand Rapids, MI: Baker Book House, 1987), 123.

10   See Catherine Drinker Bowen, *Miracle At Philadelphia: The Story of the Constitutional Convention May to September 1787* (Boston: Little, Brown & Co., 1966), ix.

11   Cited in *Miracle At Philadelphia* , 279.

12   *The Debates in the Federal Convention of 1787 Which Framed the Constitution of the United States of America*, Reported by James Madison, A Delegate from the State of Virginia (Greenwood Press Publishers, Westport, Connecticut), p. 187.

Chapter 3 — The Genius of the United States Constitution

1   John Jay, "Federalist #2," in *The Federalist Papers*, ed. Garry Wills (New York: Bantam Books, 1982), 9.

2   "'Books That Shaped America' Exhibition to Open June 25," *Library of Congress*, June 21, 2012 (REVISED July 2, 2012), https://www.loc.gov/item/prn-12-123/ (accessed October 18, 2017).

3   James Madison, "Federalist #51," in *The Federalist Papers*, ed. Garry Wills (New York: Bantam Books, 1982), 262.

4   Alexander Hamilton, "Federalist #23," in *The Federalist Papers*, ed. Garry Wills (New York: Bantam Books, 1982), 112, 113.

5   James Madison, *Notes of Debates in the Federal Convention of 1787* (New York: W. W. Norton, Inc., 1987), 78.

6   Ibid., 86.

7   Ibid., 542.

8   Madison, *Notes of Debates in the Federal Convention of 1787*, 29.

9   Madison, "Federalist #10," in *The Federalist Papers*, 49.

10   James Madison's Resolutions of the 1798 In the [Virginia] House of Delegates, *The Writings of James Madison*, Vol. 6, ed. Gaillard Hunt (New York: G. P. Putnam's Sons, 1906), 326, 327-328.

11   Joseph Story, *Commentaries on the Constitution of the United States*, Vol. III, Book III, Ch. XXXVIII, § 1697 (Boston, Hilliard, Gray and Company, 1833), 573.

Chapter 4 — A History of the Separation of Church & State

1   Robert Merrill Bartlett, *The Pilgrim Way* (Philadelphia: A Pilgrim Press Book, 1971), 54.

2   Daniel Webster, an oration at Plymouth, Massachusetts, December 22, 1820, Daniel Webster, *The Works of Daniel Webster*, vol.1 (Boston: Little, Brown and Company, 1853), 22.

3   George Bancroft, *History of the United States of America*, vol. 1 (1834), 318.

4   James Russell Lowell, *Literary Essays*, vol. 2, *New England Two Centuries Ago*. Quoted in Charles Fadiman, ed., *The American Treasury* (NY: Harper & Brothers, Publishers, 1955), 119.

5   Quoted in Lynn R. Buzzard and Samuel Ericsson, *The Battle for Religious Liberty*

(Elgin, IL: David C. Cook, 1982), 51.

6   Roger Williams, "A Plea for Religious Liberty," (1644), <http://www.constitution. org/bcp/religlib.html> (31 January 2003).

7   "Constitution of the United States of America–Analysis and Interpretation," prepared by the Legislative Reference Service of the Library of Congress, ed. Edward S. Corwin(U.S. Government Printing Office, Washington, 1953), 758,

8   John K. Wilson, "Religion Under the State Constitutions 1776–1800," *Journal of Church and State*, 32, no. 4 (fall 1990), 754.

9   Congressman James Meacham (VT), House Judiciary Committee report, March 27, 1854 (Journal of the U.S. House, 33rd Congress).

10 William J. Federer, *The Original 13: A Documentary History of Religion in America's First Thirteen States* (St. Louis, MO: Amerisearch, Inc.).

11 "Constitution of the United States" op.cit.

12 John Bouvier, *Law Dictionary* (Philadelphia: J.B. Lippincott Co., 1889).

13 James H. Landman, director of community programs for the American Bar Association Division for Public Education in Chicago, wrote in "Trying Beliefs: The Law of Cultural Orthodoxy and Dissent" (*Insights on Law and Society*, American Bar Association Division for Public Education, 2, no. 2 (winter 2002).

Chapter 5 — The State of Religious Liberty in Modern America

1   Letter from John Adams to Thomas Jefferson (28 June 1813), from Quincy, in *The Adams-Jefferson Letters: The Complete Correspondence Between Thomas Jefferson and Abigail and John Adams* (ed., Lester J. Cappon; University of North Carolina Press: Chapel Hill, NC, 1988), 338-340 <http://www.constitution.org/ primarysources/adamsprinciples.html> (10 July 2003).

2   Robert H. Bork, *Slouching Toward Gomorrah: Modern Liberalism and American Decline* (New York: Regan Books, an imprint of HarperCollins Publishers, 1996), 111.

3   Bork, *Slouching Toward Gomorrah*, 105.

Chapter 6 — The Bible and Life

1   Mother Teresa, "Whatsoever You Do . . .", Speech to the National Prayer Breakfast, Washington, DC, 3 February 1994, http://www.priestsforlife.org/brochures/mt-speech.html

2   http://www.inthefaith.com/archives/001330.php

3   http://www.punkvoter.com/guest/guest_detail.php?GuestColumnID=17

4   Warren Throckmorton, "I Had An Abortion," August 15, 2004 http://www.

townhall.com/columnists/GuestColumns/Throckmorton20040815.shtml

5   Cal Thomas, *Uncommon Sense,* (Brentwood, TN: Wolgemuth & Hyatt, 1990), 5.

6   Byron White, dissent in *Roe v. Wade,* U.S. Supreme Court, January 22, 1973.

7   Transcript of an interview with Michael Farris on location in Washington, DC (Ft. Lauderdale, FL: Coral Ridge Ministries-TV, 1996).

8   Norma McCorvey passed away on February 18, 2017.

9   Norma McCorvey with Gary Thomas, *Won by Love* (Nashville, TN: Thomas Nelson, Inc., 1997).

10   William J. Brennan, *The Abortion Holocaust* (St. Louis, MO: Landmark Press, 1983), 123.

11   "Late-Term Abortion" *OperationRescue.org,* http://www.operationrescue.org/about-abortion/late-term-abortion/ (accessed October 31, 2017).

12   Transcript from Coral Ridge Ministries TV interview with Carol Everett.

Chapter 7 — The Incarceration of America

1   Vikrant Reddy (Edited by Yuval Levin and Ramesh Ponnuru) 2015. "A New Agenda for Criminal Justice." Conservative Reform Network; Principled, practical solutions. (2015), 7.

2   Marvin Olasky, Southern Equip. Lecture 2:"Prodigal Doctrines: Going beyond "Social Justice" to "Righteous Justice"" (Audio) http://equip.sbts.edu/norton/prodigal-doctrines-going-beyond-social-justice-to-righteous-justice/

3   Adam Carrington, Christ/Popculture. Marvin Olasky and Social Justice. April 7, 2010, https://christandpopculture.com/marvin-olasky-and-social-justice/

4   Constitutional Rights Foundation, *Bill of Rights in Action,* 4, no. 3 (summer 1998), http://www.crf-usa.org/bill-of-rights-in-action/bria-14-3-a-how-welfare-began-in-the-united-states.html

5   State of the Union address of Franklin D. Roosevelt before Congress on January 4, 1935. http://stateoftheunion.onetwothree.net/texts/19350104.html

6   Robert Higgs, *The Great Society's War on Poverty.* Wednesday, September 21, 2011, https://fee.org/articles/the-great-societys-war-on-poverty/

7   Michael D. Tanner and Charles Hughes, "War on Poverty Turns 50: Are We Winning Yet?" *Policy Analysis,* no. 761, October 20, 2014.

8   Charles Murray, *Losing Ground: American Social Policy, 1950 - 1980* (New York: Basic Books, 1984).

9   Welfare: http://legal-dictionary.thefreedictionary.com/a+Brief+History+of+Welfare+Reform

10   National Center for Policy Analysis. "How to Avoid Poverty and Enter the

American Middle Class." November 6, 2009 http://www.ncpa.org/sub/dpd/index.php?Article_ID=18651

11   Michael D. Waggoner, "When the Court Took on Prayer and the Bible in Public Schools," *ReligionandPolitics.org*, June 25, 2012, http://religionandpolitics.org/2012/06/25/when-the-court-took-on-prayer-the-bible-and-public-schools/

12   National Center for Health Statistics. Out-of-wedlock childbearing has risen over the past several decades. SOURCE: CDC/NCHS, National Vital Statistics System (2012). https://www.census.gov/newsroom/cspan/childbearing/20120817_cspan_childbearing_slides.pdf

13   Robert Rector, "Marriage: America's Greatest Weapon Against Child Poverty," September 5, 2012, http://www.heritage.org/poverty-and-inequality/report/marriage-americas-greatest-weapon-against-child-poverty

14   Mitch Behna, "The Economic Effect of Abortion: Billions and Billions Lost." *LifeNews.com*. Opinion. .Jul 16, 2012 Washington, DC. http://www.lifenews.com/2012/07/16/the-economic-effect-of-abortion-billions-and-billions-lost/

15   Steven Ertelt, "Abortion Effect: usus Seeing Slowest Population Growth Since 1930," *LifeNews.com*, December 31, 2012, http://www.lifenews.com/2012/12/31/abortion-effect-u-s-seeing-slowest-population-growth-since-1930/

16   Nathan James, "The Federal Prison Population Buildup: Options for Congress." Congressional Research Service (May 20, 2016), 2. The Federal Bureau of Prisons budget is enormous, at nearly 7.5 billion dollars.

17   Kim Hunt, Steven and Robert Dumville, "Recidivism Among Federal Offenders: A Comprehensive Overview." United States Sentencing Commission (May 2016), 3.

18   The purpose of incarceration is four-fold: retribution, incapacitation, deterrence, and rehabilitation. With a nearly 50 percent recidivism rate we are failing in at least two areas.

19   Lauren E. Glaze and Laura M. Maruschak, "Parents in Prison and Their Minor Children." Bureau of Justice Statistics Special Report NCJ 222984 usus Department of Justice Office of Justice Programs (August 2008-revised March 30, 2010), 1.

20   James M. Conway and Edward T. Jones. "Seven out of Ten? Not Even Close: A Review of Research on the Likelihood of Children with Incarcerated Parents Becoming Justice Involved." Central Connecticut State University, 2015.

21   Glaze, 7.

Chapter 8 — America's Need for God

1   Psalm 11:3.

2   William J. Federer, *America's God and Country: Encyclopedia of Quotations* (St.

Louis, MO: Amerisearch, 2000), 248-249.

3   Ibid., 249.

4   Ibid.

5   Ibid., 250.

6   Paul Harvey, "God Knows Now!," *Paul Harvey News,* February 10, 1996, Copyright 1996 Paul Harvey Products, Inc., Distributed by Creators Syndicate, Inc., Los Angeles.

7   D. James Kennedy, "The Christian View of Politics" (Ft. Lauderdale: Coral Ridge Ministries, 1975), a pamphlet. Note: this is his prayer at the end of the sermon. I slightly changed the words, from prayer to prose.

8   Proverbs 29:18, KJV

9   Paul Johnson, *A History of the American People* (New York: Harper Collins Publishers, 1997), 204.

10   Cotton Mather, *The Great Works of Christ in America: Magnalia Christi Americana,* vol. 1 (Edinburgh: The Banner of Truth Trust, 1702 / 1853 / 1979), 63.

11   John Adams to Abigail Adams, April 26, 1777, Familiar Letters, 265. Quoted in Caroline Thomas Harnsberger, ed., *Treasury of Presidential Quotations* (Chicago: Follett Publishing Company, 1964), 106.

12   Theodore Roosevelt, 1916; *Works, XVIII,* 199, Caroline Thomas Harnsberger, ed., *Treasury of Presidential Quotations* (Chicago: Follett Publishing Company, 1964), 117.

13   John Quincy Adams, "In reply to an inquiry as to his unpopular stance against slavery," in David Barton, *The WallBuilder Report* (Aledo, TX: WallBuilder Press, Summer 1993), 3.

14   The original title is "Can An Empire Rise Without His Aid?"

Chapter 9 — A New Era of Cultural Engagement

1   Lee Williams, *No Room for Doubt* (Nashville, TN: Broadman Press, 1977), 36.

Appendix — National Proclamations of Prayer

1   Edward Winslow, *Young's Chronicles,* p. 350. Peter Marshall and David Manuel, *The Glory of America* (Bloomington, MN: Garborg's Heart'N Home, Inc., 1991), 10.18.

2   Virginia, Commonwealth of, 1668. Benjamin Franklin Morris, *The Christian Life and Character of the Civil Institutions of the United States* (Philadelphia, PA: L. Johnson & Co., 1863; George W. Childs, 1864), 233.

3   Robert Carter Nicholas, May 24, 1773, in a proposal for a Day of Prayer and Fasting in response to the British closing of the port at Boston. (H.B. Journal, 1773-76, 124). Douglas Southall Freeman, *George Washington*, 6 Vol. (NY: Charles Scribner's Sons, 1948-54), Vol. III, 350.

4   Jonathan Trumbull, April 19, 1775, as Governor of the Connecticut Colony proclaiming a day of fasting and prayer. Verna M. Hall, *The Christian History of the American Revolution* (San Francisco: Foundation for American Christian Education, 1976), 407.

5   Continental Congress. June 12, 1775. *The Journals of the Continental Congress* 1774-1789, vol. 2 (Washington, D.C.: Government Printing Office, 1905), Vol. II, 87.

6   Continental Congress, March 16, 1776, passed a resolution declaring May 17, 1776, as a National Day of Humiliation, Fasting and Prayer, presented by General William Livingston. *Journals of Congress*, p. 93. *The Journals of the Continental Congress*, 1774-1789, vol. 4 (Washington, D.C.: Government Printing Office, 1905), Vol. IV.

7   George Washington, May 15, 1776, in his issued orders, Jared Sparks, ed., *The Writings of George Washington*, vol. 3 (Boston American Stationer's Company, 1837; NY: F. Andrew's, 1834-1847), 392.

8   Abraham Lincoln, "Proclamation for a National Day of Fasting," March 30, 1863 in Marion Mills Miller, ed., *Life and Works of Abraham Lincoln Centenary Edition*, vol. 6 (New York: The Current Literature Publishing Co., 1907), 156-157.

9   United States Congress, June 17, 1952, President Harry S. Truman issued Proclamation 2978, declaring a National Day of Prayer.

10 United States Congress, January 25, 1988 in the Second Session of the One Hundredth Congress. Public Law 100-307 - May 5, 1988 [Legislative History - S. 1378]; May 5, 1988. 36 USC 169th, Congressional Record, Vol. 134 (1988), Apr.22, considered and passed Senate, May 2, considered and passed House. 102 STAT. 456.

ACKNOWLEGMENTS

There are a number of people who must be thanked for this project. Without them it would never have come to be. First of all, I thank Dr. John Sorensen, who initially came up with the idea for the project and its title. I'm also grateful for his contribution of an inspiring chapter. I'm also grateful for Debbie Revitzer who served as his liaison to me for this writing assignment. I thank my good friend, Bill Federer, who generously let us use some of his writings for this project, including the Introduction and Appendix, as well as a chapter on the separation of church and state. I also thank Dr. Peter Lillback, the president of Providence Forum (with whom I had the privilege of co-writing the national best-seller, *George Washington's Sacred Fire*), for letting us use a key portion of his book, *Freedom's Holy Light: With a Firm Reliance on Divine Providence*. We are most grateful to Jerry Nordskog, publisher of *The Book That Made America,* which shows the contributions of the Bible to our nation, for letting us use a chapter from that book in this volume. I also thank Dr. Frank Wright, president and CEO of D. James Kennedy Ministries, not only for his insightful chapter here, but also for his vision to see this project through. Furthermore, thanks go as well to Dr. Linda Smith and The Honorable John Hostettler of the D. James Kennedy Center for Christian Statesmanship for their worthy additions to this book. We're also grateful to the legacy of Dr. D. James Kennedy, whose moral voice on the issues of the day is still sorely needed in our day. I'm also very grateful to Dr. Karen Gushta for her superb job with the editing of the manuscript. Finally, I thank my Lord and Savior Jesus Christ, to whom every word of this book is dedicated, with the prayer that He uses it as He sees fit for His honor and glory.

Jerry Newcombe, D. Min.
Ft. Lauderdale, Florida
November 8, in the Year of our Lord 2017

INDEX

ABOUT THE AUTHORS

David Gibbs, III is the president and general counsel of the National Center for Life and Liberty (NCLL.org), a ministry organization that defends life and liberty freedoms nationwide. Mr. Gibbs speaks regularly to audiences in churches and conferences while also litigating cases as a trial attorney. He has authored five books including *Fighting for Dear Life: The Untold Story of Terri Schiavo* and *Understanding the Constitution*. Attorney Gibbs graduated from Duke Law School and manages the Gibbs Law Firm with offices in Dallas, Texas; St. Petersburg, Florida; and Washington, D.C. He is admitted to practice before the United States Supreme Court and numerous federal circuit and district courts nationwide. He has also been admitted to the State Bars of Florida, Minnesota, Colorado, North Dakota, Ohio, Texas, Tennessee, Michigan, and the District of Columbia. Mr. Gibbs is a frequent spokesperson on radio and television having appeared on many major news and talk programs.

William J. Federer is a nationally known speaker, bestselling author, and president of Amerisearch, Inc., (AmericanMinute.com), a publishing company dedicated to researching America's noble heritage. He is author of *America's God and Country,* which has been cited by the U. S. Supreme Court (*Greece v. Galloway,* 2014). Among his many books, his most recent is, *Who Is the King in America? and Who Are the Counselors to the King?: An Overview of 6,000 Years of History and Why America Is Unique.* Mr. Federer is also host of the Faith In History television program on the TCT network and the daily radio feature, American Minute, which is broadcast across America and by the internet. Bill has appeared on numerous television programs, including CSPAN, Hannity & Colmes, the O'Reilly Factor, the Coral Ridge Hour and Truths That Transform. He has also been interviewed on thousands of radio programs, including Focus on the Family, Judicial Watch, Michael Medved, and many others. As a speaker,

Bill has spoken across America at events ranging from the Federalist Society to local Jaycee and Rotary Clubs. He has been awarded several honorary doctorates: an Honorary Doctorate of Humanities from American Christian College in 2004 and an Honorary Doctorate of Global Leadership from Midwest University in 2013.

The Honorable John Hostettler is senior executive director of the Center for Christian Statesmanship in Washington, D.C. (Statesman. org). He served six terms in the United States House of Representatives, representing the Eighth District of Indiana in southwest and west central Indiana from 1995 to 2007. While in office, he served on the House Judiciary Committee (among others). Prior to his service in Congress, John was enlightened and inspired by the teaching of Dr. D. James Kennedy—especially Dr. Kennedy's radio ministry, Truths That Transform. Moreover, it was at the first Reclaiming America for Christ Conference at Coral Ridge Presbyterian Church that soon-to-be-candidate-for-Congress John Hostettler heard Dr. Kennedy's admonition, "Some of you ought to be in office!" Less than a year later, Citizen John Hostettler became Congressman John Hostettler. Congressman Hostettler holds a Bachelor of Science degree in Mechanical Engineering from Rose-Hulman Institute of Technology in Terre Haute, Indiana. He is author of *Ordained and Established: A Statesman-Citizen's Guide to the United States Constitution.*

D. James Kennedy, M.Div., M.Th., D.D., D.Sac.Lit., Ph.D., Litt.D., D.Sac.Theol., D.HumaneLet. (1930-2007), was the most listened-to Presbyterian minister in history because of his internationally syndicated television and radio broadcasts. In 2005, Dr. Kennedy was inducted into the National Religious Broadcasters' Hall of Fame. For 47 years, he was the senior pastor of Coral Ridge Presbyterian Church in Fort Lauderdale, Florida, where he launched the world-wide personal evangelism training ministry, Evangelism Explosion International, which by 1996 was in every nation of the world. Dr. Kennedy authored 70 books, including the bestsellers, *Evangelism Explosion, Why I*

Believe, and (with Jerry Newcombe) *What If Jesus Had Never Been Born?* In addition to founding the ministry of Evangelism Explosion International, which contributed to the exponential growth of Coral Ridge Presbyterian Church, Dr. Kennedy also founded the ministries of Coral Ridge Ministries Media, (now D. James Kennedy Ministries), Knox Theological Seminary, Westminster Academy, the Center for Christian Statesmanship, and the Center for Reclaiming America.

Peter Lillback, Th.M., Ph.D., is founder and president of Providence Forum, (ProvidenceForum.org), and president and professor of historical theology and church history at Westminster Theological Seminary in Philadelphia. He also serves as senior editor of the new *Unio cum Christo: An International Journal of Reformed Theology and Life*. His books include the national bestseller, *George Washington's Sacred Fire* (with Jerry Newcombe), *Wall of Misconception, Freedom's Holy Light: With A Firm Reliance On Divine Providence*, as well as *A Theological Guide to Calvin's Institutes: Essays and Analysis*, co-edited with David Hall.

Jerry Newcombe, D. Min., serves as senior producer and on-air-host and columnist for D. James Kennedy Ministries. He has produced or co-produced more than 60 one-hour national television specials for D. James Kennedy Ministries (formerly Coral Ridge Ministries) and is the author or co-author of 29 books, including two bestsellers, *What If Jesus Had Never Been Born* (with Dr. D. James Kennedy) and *George Washington's Sacred Fire* (with Dr. Peter Lillback). Jerry has also been a guest on numerous talk shows including Janet Parshall's America, Politically Incorrect with Bill Maher, Point of View, and the Fox News Channel. He writes a weekly opinion column that is hosted by D. James Kennedy Ministries and several online publications (see: JerryNewcombe.com).

Linda W. Smith, Ph.D., is the president of the D. James Kennedy Center for Christian Statesmanship (Statesman.org). Previously she served as executive vice president and chief operating officer for National Religious Broadcasters; chief of the Office of Public Affairs for the Federal Bureau of Prisons; and chief of staff for the U.S. Parole Commission. As chief of public affairs, Linda oversaw congressional, media, and public relations for the Federal Bureau of Prisons. At the U.S. Parole Commission, she served as chief analyst for the National Appellate Board and other positions before assuming the role as chief of staff, overseeing this multi-mission agency, responsible for the release and re-arrest of federal offenders. Linda received her doctorate in Public Administration from the University of Southern California. She holds a master's degree in Public Administration from the same school, and a second master's degree and a Bachelor of Arts from West Virginia University. She is a member of the steering committee of American Christian Leaders for Israel.

John B. Sorenson, M.A., D.D., D.HumaneLet., is president of Evangelism Explosion International (EvangelismExplosion.org), a ministry dedicated to equipping and training believers worldwide to witness for Jesus Christ. John received his training in EE in 1991, and subsequently he joined the staff of EE International, first serving as director for ministry advancement and then as executive vice president. In 2008, the Board of Directors voted to appoint John as the president of EE International, an office previously held exclusively by EE's founder, Dr. D. James Kennedy. John has written *Your Story Counts,* and co-authored with Dr. D. James Kennedy, *Well Done: A Christian Doctrine of Works.* He is the host of the daily radio feature Share Life Today on the Moody Radio Network.

Frank Wright, Ph.D., serves as the president and chief executive officer of D. James Kennedy Ministries (DJKM.org). Dr. Wright was a decade's long friend and student of Dr. D. James Kennedy and he shares an understanding of Dr. Kennedy's Biblical perspective, and his commitment to the Great Commission of Jesus Christ and the Biblical imperative of the Cultural Mandate. Dr. Kennedy named

Dr. Wright as the first director of the D. James Kennedy Center for Christian Statesmanship in Washington, D.C. Later Dr. Wright served as the president and chief executive officer of the National Religious Broadcasters, as well as president and chief operating officer of Salem Media Group, one of the preeminent Christian media companies in the world. Dr. Wright has written *The Road Back to Sanity: Finding Our Way Home from Cultural Delusion,* and co-authored *Making Your Life Count: Discover God's Plan for the Rest of Your Life* (with Karen VanTil Gushta, Jerry Newcombe, and John Rabe).